A Guide to EHR Adoption: Implementation Through Organizational Transformation

Cynthia Davis, MHSA, RN, and Marcy Stoots, MS, RN-BC

HIMSS Mission
To lead healthcare transformation through the effective use of health information technology.

Printed in the U.S.A.   5 4 3 2 1

Requests for permission to make copies of any part of this work should be sent to:
Permissions Editor
HIMSS
33 W. Monroe St., #1700
Chicago, IL 60603-5616
nvitucci@himss.org

ISBN: 978-0-9844577-9-3

For more information about HIMSS, please visit www.himss.org.

About the Authors

Cynthia Davis MHSA, RN, is a recognized technology adoption leader and strategist with more than 30 years of experience in nursing and healthcare administration in academic medical centers and community-based health systems. She is the co-founding Principal with CIC Advisory, a clinician-led informatics consulting services firm that specializes in analytics, implementation, optimization, strategic planning, executive coaching, and American Recovery and Reinvestment Act (ARRA)/Meaningful Use Readiness (see www.cicadvisory.com).

Previously, Ms. Davis was Vice President of Clinical Transformation at BayCare Health System in Florida, with responsibility for strategic planning, implementation, and ongoing support of BayCare's clinical applications. She also led the development of technology and processes for the first planned digital hospital in Georgia. Under her leadership, EHR implementations have high rates of physician and clinician adoption and satisfaction that result in streamlined patient care processes and improved clinical outcomes. Ms. Davis, who began her career as a nurse, has facilitated collaborative partnership initiatives involving informatics research between community health systems.

Her passion for improving healthcare quality and safety has led to the development of an accountable, technology-enabled transformation methodology with demonstrated results and improvements in the process of clinical decision making and care delivery process. She is a national speaker on the topic of healthcare transformation, clinical adoption, and benefits realization.

Ms. Davis received her master's degree in Health Services Administration from the University of Michigan and her bachelor's degree in Nursing from the University of New Mexico. She is a fellow with the American College of Healthcare Executives.

Marcy Stoots, MS, RN-BC, is a transformation leader with specialization in the application of EHR tools that improve the quality and safety of healthcare delivery. She is the co-founding Principal of CIC Advisory, a clinician-led informatics consulting services firm that specializes in analytics, implementation, optimization, strategic planning, executive coaching, and ARRA/Meaningful Use Readiness (see www.cicadvisory.com).

Previously, Ms. Stoots served as EHR Director for BayCare Health System in Florida, where she led a successful clinical transformation in the implementation and optimization of this large-scale integrated delivery network's EHR. She has worked on several multi-million dollar EHR initiatives for other organizations, including the National Institutes of Health Clinical Center in Bethesda, Maryland.

As a former emergency department and pediatric critical care nurse, Ms. Stoots witnessed near-miss medical events that could have been prevented. She is a frequent speaker to groups such as the Summer Institute in Nursing Informatics and the American Congress of Healthcare Executives on her unique methodology to implement and optimize technology tools that substantially improve the safety of patient care.

Ms. Stoots holds a Master of Science degree in Nursing Informatics from the University of Maryland in Baltimore and an undergraduate degree in Nursing from Virginia Commonwealth University, as well as American Nurse Credentialing Center certification in Nursing Informatics. She is pursing a Doctor of Nursing Practice degree at Vanderbilt University, with a focus in Nursing and Clinical Informatics. She is investigating EHR safety risks and developing a safety strategy and toolkit for organizations as they implement and optimize their EHRs.

Case Study Contributors

Robert Collins is a talented, results-oriented healthcare information technology leader with 21 years of experience and an outstanding record of accomplishments in clinical transformation, strategy planning, project management, and information technology leadership for small rural hospitals and large urban hospitals. As President of NEOS Technologies, Mr. Collins and his team assist hospitals and ambulatory clinics in transitioning from paper records to electronic records to achieve best practices workflow to leverage EHRs for safe, efficient, effective patient care and to contain the rising expenses associated with providing care. Mr. Collins currently serves on various health information technology special interest groups including regional health information exchanges, electronic health records, and computerized provider order entry. He serves on the Computer Sciences Advisory Board at Georgia Southwestern State University and Darton College.

Jesse Diaz, MBA, CPHIMS, is Vice President and Chief Information Officer at Phoebe Putney Health System in Albany, Georgia. In his position as CIO, Mr. Diaz is responsible for IT strategy development and implementation at all of the Phoebe Health System facilities including the implementation of their EHR for inpatient and ambulatory sites. Mr. Diaz graduated from Troy University in 1984 with a bachelor of science degree in accounting and in 1988 with a master's degree in business administration. He spent 22 years at his previous hospital in various IT roles, which culminated in his promotion to Director of Information Systems. He was recruited to his current role in 2006.

Susan Heichert, BSN, MA, FHIMSS, is Senior Vice President/Chief Information Officer at Allina Hospitals and Clinics in Minneapolis, Minnesota, where she was part of the team that implemented an EHR. She received her bachelor's degree in Nursing from the University of Maryland and a master's degree from the University of Minnesota. Ms. Heichert has been working in healthcare for more 30 years in various capacities.

Ryan Kennedy is an IT Project Manager within the Department of Clinical Research Informatics (DCRI) at the National Institutes of Health Clinical Center in Bethesda, Maryland, as well as a part-time instructor for the University of Maryland School of Nursing. His background includes several years of configuration management experience, spanning across multiple government agencies and public hospital systems. As lead of the DCRI Project Management Office, Mr. Kennedy's project successes have contributed to the implementation of new clinical systems and improved workflow processes.

Mary Lambert, MBA, RHIA, is Director of Clinical Decision Support and Optimization at Allina Hospitals and Clinics, Minneapolis, Minnesota. Ms. Lambert led the Process Integration team on the Allina EHR Project Implementation team. She has a bachelor's degree in Health Information from the College of St. Scholastica, and a master's degree in business administration from the University of St. Thomas. Her background includes positions in health information operations management, revenue cycle improvement, project management, systems implementation, and clinical decision support.

Alastair MacGregor, MB ChB, is Senior Vice President, Chief Medical Information Officer, and Chief Information Officer at Methodist Le Bonheur Healthcare in Memphis, Tennessee. Dr. MacGregor is responsible for all medical, nursing, ancillary information, business, and human resources systems teams that contribute to all aspects of the EHR, from procurement to implementation, adoption, and maintenance in the acute and ambulatory venues. He received a MB ChB (MD degree equivalent) from the University of Glasgow, Scotland. Dr. MacGregor is a member of the Royal College of General Practitioners of the United Kingdom (board certification in family medicine). His formal medical career was in anesthesiology/critical care and family medicine.

Kristen O'Shea, MS, RN, NEA-BC, is Vice President of Patient Care Services at Gettysburg Hospital in Gettysburg, Pennsylvania, and is the Clinical Transformation Officer for WellSpan Health in York, Pennsylvania. In her hybrid role at WellSpan, Ms. O'Shea leads innovation and clinical change related to the implementation of the EHR. As CNO at Gettysburg Hospital, she led the nursing team to develop highly reliable care with consistently strong and award-winning performance.

Ms. O'Shea graduated from the University of Pittsburgh with a Bachelor of Science degree in nursing and the University of Maryland with a Master of Science degree in Nursing. She is the editor of the book *Staff Development Nursing Secrets* and author of articles on device connectivity and infusion management.

Jane Renwick, MSA, BSN, RN-BC, NEA-BC, is Director of Enterprise Applications at Trinity Health in Novi, Michigan. Ms. Renwick's responsibilities include providing strategic executive clinical leadership for Genesis, an initiative that integrates leading-edge technology to support the delivery of high-quality patient care, providing clinical and information services consultation to internal and external customers, and leading and consulting for clinical technology solutions throughout the continuum of care. She received her Bachelor of Science degree in Nursing from the University of Michigan and a Master of Science degree in Health Care Administration from Central Michigan University.

Patricia P. Sengstack, DNP, RN-BC, CPHIMS, is the Deputy Chief Information Officer and Chief of Clinical Informatics at the NIH Clinical Center in Bethesda, Maryland. She recently received her Doctor of Nursing Practice degree from Vanderbilt University and has a master's degree in Nursing Informatics from the University of Maryland. Dr. Sengstack has worked as a consultant at Computer Sciences Corporation and assisted in the implementation of the Clinical Center's EHR. Her nursing background includes working as an ICU nurse and a Clinical Nurse Specialist in the Washington, DC metropolitan area. Dr. Sengstack has contributed to multiple publications, the most recent being an article in the *Journal of Healthcare Information Management* on the configuration of safe computerized provider order entry (CPOE) systems. She has presented at the local and national level in multiple venues to share her informatics experience and knowledge. Her focus over the last several years has been on building a program to improve the evaluation process of IT systems, along with evaluating methods to ensure IT safety.

Sarah Shultz, MS, RN-BC, CCRN, is Clinical Informatics Coordinator for St. Joseph Hospital in Kokomo, Indiana, where she has partnered with another lead RN and the clinical leadership team to implement the EHR in phases. As her hospital is part of St. Vincent Health, Ms. Shultz also networks with colleagues throughout her healthcare system to meet organizational objectives. She is an adjunct professor for Anderson University for undergraduate and graduate Nursing Informatics classes. Ms. Shultz holds a Master of Science degree in Nursing from the University of Southern Indiana and is certified by the American Nurse Credentialing Center in Nursing Informatics.

Dedication

For all the victims of mismanaged healthcare and medical errors who died or suffered needlessly, and for all those future patients who will benefit from higher quality care.

Acknowledgements

We would like to thank Lindsey P. Jarrell for providing the foreword to this book. A highly accomplished healthcare leader with more than 16 years of experience, Mr. Jarrell has an exceptional record of achievement in consulting leadership, clinical transformation, strategic planning, and CIO leadership. He has held top executive positions in fast-growth healthcare IT consulting firms of 600+ consultants and large integrated delivery networks of 11 hospitals and 18,000+ employees. He has a track record of success and integrity in health IT. Mr. Jarrell recently co-authored a book titled *Consumer-Centric Healthcare: Opportunities and Challenges for Providers* published by Health Administration Press. In 2009 he was the recipient of the CHIME-AHA Transformational Leader of the Year award.

Special thanks goes to Jill Max for editing the manuscript. Ms. Max is a freelance science and health writer who holds a master's degree from the Columbia University Graduate School of Journalism, where she completed a concentration in health and science. She has written articles, white papers, web content and book chapters on a wide variety of topics in medicine, health, and environmental science. Most recently she has written on topics related to health IT and is a regular contributor to various publications produced by the Yale University School of Medicine. Ms. Max is the recipient of a 2010 Award of Excellence from the Association of American Medical Colleges.

We would also like to thank Joe Bohn for his diligent effort and review of our manuscript.

Most importantly, we would like to thank our husbands, Wright Davis and Stan Stoots, for giving us the time and space to work on this book, and for all of their support on so many ventures over the years.

Table of Contents

List of Figures and Tables

Figures

Tables

Foreword

By Lindsey P. Jarrell

We have seen an incredible rise in health information technology within the United States in the last twenty years and the wave of new implementations with even more impressive technology and software is only beginning to get underway. Not only are the projects becoming more expensive, but the time lines are compressing and the scale is getting much larger. Large-scale projects within hospitals and health systems require courage, determination, money, intelligence, and a deep understanding of people—patients, clinicians, and administrative management.

I have had the privilege of working with the authors of this book during very large health system transformation projects. During those times, we dreamed up plans, formed teams, created budgets, hit brick walls, celebrated success, failed, and, ultimately, learned an incredible amount about what it takes to transform the way an organization utilizes technology and how people react during episodes of massive change.

I distinctly remember the first go-live of more than twenty that were planned for the next five years within a large health system where I worked. The chief operating officer of one of the large hospitals within the system had come to witness that morning's go-live event before the next go-live at his hospital. He pulled me aside and shared how impressed he was with the go-live event, including the user satisfaction and process improvements he observed. It was at this moment that the light went on for him and his team as to why methodical preparation, communication, change management, and project management was so important. Many times when we are working on very large projects with teams that have limited experience, we find it hard to explain why certain steps, techniques, and methodologies are useful. This book can help you in that journey.

The concepts and ideas presented in this book work very well. They have been proven repeatedly in systems across the United States and have been used to introduce change in both large and small organizations. Previously, as CIO of a health system, I saw these tools and techniques work across all levels of the organization and now, as a Principal with PwC, I work with health systems throughout the country and see many that have yet to embrace change management, planning, and communication as the tenets of a successful transformation.

Healthcare and its level of quality are highly personal to me. I lost my mom to cancer when I was twenty years old. I served as her care navigator, question asker, and lead defender during her year-long battle with cancer. That experience drives me everyday to create a better healthcare experience for patients and families across the continuum of care. I know the co-authors of this book have similar stories and an incredible drive to improve care for patients and their families. Their experience and passion for capturing knowledge and lessons learned means that we can all learn from past work on large-scale transformation initiatives. As we move into a new era of larger and larger clinical system implementations, including ones on a national scale, we can utilize this work to improve the outcomes of our projects and teams.

Introduction

There is no higher calling among hospitals than to take good and safe care of patients. Early in her career as a nurse, one of us (Cynthia Davis) had an experience that left an indelible impression. This is her story:

I was working in an extremely busy ICU in Albuquerque, New Mexico. Each new day seemed more chaotic than the one before and presented complex challenges, as well as opportunities. I was the charge nurse on the unit and all twenty beds were filled with exceedingly ill or badly injured patients.

While on shift one day, I received a call from one of the surgical residents whom I knew well. He said, "We screwed up. We need a bed right away." My immediate thought was, "We don't have any beds, we're filled to capacity, and we can't move anyone out of the unit." The resident told me that a young man had arrived for an outpatient procedure and had been expected to depart that same day. But something had gone wrong in the operating room for Chris, a patient who was about to come into my life.

Chris was a paraplegic who had been experiencing considerable upper back pain. His neurosurgeon had told him that a treatment involving the placement of wires in his brain would help to reduce the pain. Chris, as well as everyone else, was expecting that he would arrive for this outpatient procedure, receive the treatment, and depart that evening, feeling less pain.

When Chris entered the hospital that day, the attending nurse gathered data about his health history, medications, and allergies. A single piece of paper, which accompanied Chris into the operating room, contained all of his health information. The anesthesiologist injected medications to put Chris to sleep for the surgery, inadvertently failing to notice that Chris had an allergy to one of the medications administered.

Chris stopped breathing for nearly five minutes. Concurrently, the OR staff did not realize that Chris's heart had stopped as a result of a medical equipment failure. They were able to resuscitate him, but because he had been without oxygen for so long, he had to rely on mechanically assisted ventilation as he was wheeled into the ICU. What's worse, he was no longer merely paraplegic; he became quadriplegic and lost the use of his arms, hands, and upper body.

Further complicating matters, prior to his surgery Chris had written that he didn't wish to be resuscitated. This means that he didn't want his heart or breathing restarted in case of an emergency. In the heat of the moment, the attending doctor had resuscitated Chris. He had failed to honor the patient's wishes because the information was not readily available.

For nine months we cared for Chris, who was no longer a whole human being in mind or body. Chris suffered every kind of infection possible, including in his bladder and his lungs. He was in constant misery and ended up needing a tracheotomy simply to draw a breath.

When Chris's neurosurgeon went on a month-long vacation to Europe, I spoke to the surgical resident who was taking care of Chris. I asked, "If we take Chris off the breathing machine for a day, can he go in peace?" It was agreed that we could do that.

We worked around the clock to get Chris off of the ventilator equipment and finally, after nine months, wheeled him out of the intensive care unit. We brought him up to the nursing care unit on the medical-surgical floor. Chris lived another three days before he quietly passed away.

It's been more than thirty years, and I have not forgotten Chris. If the entire care team had known about his allergy and had possessed the proper information from his primary care physician's office, we could have alerted the anesthesiologist. This young man would have been spared his fate. To me, his story and the tragedy that befell him while he was in the hospital's care became a life-defining moment of clarity.

Not a day goes by since when I don't acknowledge that when we have a breakdown in communication, or in the patient care process, we potentially impact patients' lives in chillingly real and permanent ways.

We wrote this book to explain how, as we move into an era of high-tech and instant communication, healthcare practitioners everywhere are establishing a new foundation. This foundation allows us to take highly fragmented and decentralized healthcare delivery systems and make them better, safer, more responsive, and patient-centered—in line with aims for improving the quality of healthcare set forth by the Institute of Medicine in 2001.[1] We owe that to ourselves, and we certainly owe that to our patients.

If you seek to implement effective change within your organization, you've picked up the right book. We will describe a proven transformation process that is a microcosm of what is happening in all hospitals, physician offices, and other care delivery sites across the country. We will help you build the foundation of a methodology that contributes to the deliberate care that both delights patients and prevents errors like those that happened to Chris.

In this book, we want to help you embrace the concept of consistency, or what we call *systemness*. Initially, many hospitals and physician practices grapple with the same issue, and many organizations struggle to practice to systemwide evidence-based standards. At the end of Chapters 1 through 9, we have provided a set of insights, lessons learned, and questions termed *Thinking Forward*. As you finish your reading, the questions simply serve as a reminder of key issues to consider as you move forward with your own implementations. As a result of delving into this book, you will gain an understanding of how to increase the quality and safety of care delivered within your organization through effective change management.

Fortunately, when top leadership has a vision of uniting all components of an organization, it makes a huge difference. Others have asked us how they can embrace *systemness* within their organization and achieve widespread buy-in, as well as practice to a standard resulting in higher quality healthcare delivery that is predictable, effective, and patient-centered. *A Guide to EHR Adoption: Implementation Through Organizational Transformation* provides crucial answers.

This book is intended to provide you with an education. You're going to discover opportunities to alter your own way of thinking and new techniques and new procedures to embrace that are proven to work under the most intense implementation circumstances. We're offering you proven transformation management techniques that have been demonstrated and that work. You'll also learn how to apply these techniques to other large-scale transformation initiatives such as meeting Meaningful Use and accountable care organization (ACO) requirements as they emerge. We hope that you accept our gift.

—Cynthia Davis, MHSA, RN, and Marcy Stoots, MS, RN-BC

CHAPTER 1

At the Crossroads of Transformation

INTRODUCTION

The Health Information Technology for Economic and Clinical Health Act (HITECH), part of the American Recovery and Reinvestment Act of 2009 (ARRA),[1] was established to offer healthcare organizations and physicians financial incentives to install electronic health record (EHR) systems. The HITECH program has several goals. The first is to stimulate the economy and encourage the implementation of interoperable health information—moving patient information *with* the patient and *for the benefit* of the patient. Demonstrating the Centers for Medicare & Medicaid Services' (CMS') "Meaningful Use" of such systems[2] is a key programmatic initiative that was initiated under the HITECH Act. With the passage of the Patient Protection and Affordable Care Act of 2010[3] came a number of new initiatives that will require leveraging the full capabilities of EHRs in the years to come. New programs such as accountable care organizations, healthcare innovation zones, and comparative effectiveness research will impact our nation's health system for decades to come, and each will be enabled by the implementation of EHRs and other health information technologies.

At the outset of these healthcare transformation journeys, we know that human factors and the potential for unintended consequences, rather than technology, represent many of the implementation challenges. Likewise, your biggest job and constant challenge is managing the psychology of human change: helping people through a significant transformation process. To sustain progress and achieve enduring transformation, your frontline clinicians and physicians need to embrace the new system in their daily patient care activities.

ENJOY THE BONUS OR INCUR THE PENALTY

With Meaningful Use, whether you're a full-service provider, a physician practice, or an acute care facility, if you have a certified medical record system in place by 2016 and you're able to demonstrate through the use of your electronic system a higher-quality level of service, you'll be able to receive federally mandated financial incentives. For example, large, integrated healthcare delivery systems with multiple hospitals might receive incentive packages of more than $40 million or more over five years, depending on the number of hospitals—a significant sum. Smaller healthcare organizations could receive significant sums as well, depending on how many hospitals are within their organization. It is recommended that an organization's leadership team do a full cost benefit analysis as part of their Meaningful Use strategy in order to determine specific incentives and timing for an individual organization.

Alternatively, healthcare organizations in the same markets that have not met the criteria could face several million dollars in annual penalties. In demonstrating Meaningful Use, your EHR will have to be fully functional and achieve targeted metrics. Many of these metrics impact physicians and transform the way they do their work.

Physicians are often not enthusiastic about using computers to enter orders or structured data; they feel it reduces their productivity and impacts their abilitiy to deliver quality patient care. Yet, you will need to rely on your physicians to achieve these financial incentives to avoid the penalties.

Your transformation campaign for a higher level of care delivered is not simply good for patients; it directly contributes to your facility's profitability. Meanwhile, the clock is ticking. Thousands of patients in acute care settings are there due to healthcare industry medical errors. Victims of such errors populate hospitals, nursing homes, physicians' offices, and everywhere in between.

THE NUMBERS ARE QUIETLY STAGGERING

"To Err Is Human," a 1999 report released by the Institute of Medicine (IOM) of the National Academies, first raised awareness that the numbers of medical errors in hospitals are staggering, resulting in an estimated 44,000 to 98,000 lives lost annually.[4] A follow-up 2001 report, "Crossing the Quality Chasm," outlined the strategy and direction for improving the quality of care across the nation.[5] Despite this call to attention, the U.S. still does not deliver high-quality and consistent care to its healthcare consumers.[5]

The results of a study of U.S. hospital-acquired infections (HAI) between 1990 and 2002 was published in 2007 by the Centers for Disease Control and Prevention and indicated that an estimated 99,000 deaths occurred in 2002 as a result of 1.7 million HAIs.[6] In 2010, a study was published in the *Archives of Internal Medicine* on HAIs associated with sepsis and pneumonia from 1998 to 2006. The analysis and results of this study indicated that for 2006 alone, it was estimated that 48,000 deaths in U.S. hospitals were attributable to HAI-associated sepsis and pneumonia.[7] Even if that number was reduced by 90 percent, it would still be far too high. Data such as these represent a tragedy for the families of the victims of those fatal infections. And, remarkably, such HAIs can be reduced or even prevented just by the simple act of rigorous handwashing.

One way to address this issue is to implement a rule within an EHR to reduce sepsis. Long before a patient actually shows symptoms, the EHR is examining the data and alerting the clinicians if something isn't right. For example, vital signs data such as temperature and respiratory rate, as well as laboratory data, are analyzed based on the system's internal logic. The physician and nurse are alerted that the patient may be developing sepsis well ahead of when the caregiver might realize it. Institutions that have done this type of work have seen a dramatic decrease in mortality.

BAD HANDWRITING, BAD MEDICINE

Deciphering clinically relevant handwritten information can be quite challenging. Consider the example in Figure 1-1.

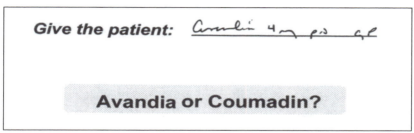

Figure 1-1: Prescription Handwriting Challenges

Much like physicians, nurses don't always have legible handwriting. They are often in a hurry, leaning over a desk or counter, and writing at the wrong angle, perhaps with the wrong utensil. In some ways, the most dangerous device in healthcare is the pen. In making hospital rounds, almost all nurses will tell you that they've prevented some near misses. Patients should not need luck or serendipity, however, to obtain the care they were intended to receive.

Currently, clinicians are forever chasing down paper charts. However, as more and more of the documentation transitions to an electronic format and as discrete data are potentially available to everyone having appropriate access, healthcare professionals and patients everywhere can benefit. The critical factor then will be that patient information is current, accurate, and available in real time.

While it's truly legitimate to be interrupted by a patient seeking his or her health information, it's quite another thing to be interrupted by members of the healthcare team or departments who are looking for information. In the paper world, the nurse is often the source of information, which is an added burden to an already full patient schedule. However, in the electronic world, all members of the healthcare team have easy and remote access to information.

REDESIGNING THE SYSTEM

The federal government has issued a strong mandate to each of us in the industry: redesign the healthcare system. What we're doing to achieve this mandate hasn't necessarily worked to the level that it could. The complexity of the system is greater than most can comprehend due to the fragmentation and decentralization of care delivery processes and the disparate individuals and organizations involved in the system. We devote enormous resources to the wrong kinds of procedures. Often, we're not providing the right type of care in the right place at the right time.

Evidence-based Medicine

The great news is that the technology to revamp healthcare is now here, waiting to be harnessed. Today's data systems allow us to leverage the knowledge that we have, draw upon the best of what else is known and what truly works, and apply this knowledge in a variety of settings. For example, *The New England Journal of Medicine* reported in a 2011 article that a group of physicians at Stanford University used data captured in their organization's EHR to drive medical decision making for a pediatric patient with systemic lupus erythematosus (SLE). In this case randomized control trials, the highest level of evidence, were not available for this particular scenario. But an electronic review of data in their data warehouse, conducted by one clinician in just a few hours, provided the necessary information that the medical team could analyze and act upon. The fact that electronic data were available to analyze and use for real-time decision making in clinical care is a leap forward and a striking example of how EHRs can propel evidence-based medicine forward.[8]

Industrywide, through the use of technology, we need to promote evidence-based practice, make it personal by focusing on the unique needs of each patient, and continue to improve overall care.

As we continue to provide care and gauge the outcomes, those outcomes are added to a knowledge base in an eternal upward spiral.

Coordination Is Critical

Because our healthcare system is currently fragmented, as a patient you could visit a primary care physician, then call on a cardiologist, then an endocrinologist, and then an orthopedic physician—and none of these providers would have the opportunity to talk with one another about your overall health. In many cases they may not want to discuss your overall health with other physicians involved in your care. Unless you are your own advocate and supply the information to them, each dispenses care without knowledge of the others.

As we rebuild the healthcare system, we must position primary care physicians at the helm to be the "captains" of the care delivery process. They need to be privy to *all* that occurs with a patient's care. This requires automation and real-time communication among all care providers. Patients, as active healthcare consumers, require more information about their own care. Offering them full transparency about their medications, options, and costs, as well as electronic access to their records, will serve to result in patients who are empowered.

IT DIFFERENCES IN HEALTHCARE

When people compare adoption of information technology (IT) in healthcare to other industries such as airline reservations or banking, it seems as if healthcare is lagging. Most healthcare functions, however, are far more complex than, say, banking.

Transaction standards for an automated teller machine (ATM) machine include 128 variables. In contrast, the Unified Medical Language System offers 6.7 million names corresponding to more than 1.3 million concepts relating to healthcare functions.[9] IT has already made the rounds when it comes to typical transactions such as charging procedures for revenue capture. Across the board within the healthcare industry, however, we're still in the formative stages of technology implementation. To move along in these formative stages, the HIMSS Analytic EMR Adoption Model[SM] (EHRAM) is used to track EHR progress at hospitals and health systems. The EHRAM scores hospitals on their progress in completing the eight stages to creating a paperless patient record environment. For example, as of the third quarter of 2011, only 13.2 percent of U.S. hospitals had achieved Stage 4, which means that these organizations have computerized provider order entry (CPOE) with clinical decision support.[10]

As a result of federal mandates, patient care and safety, and the need to remain competitive, healthcare organizations everywhere must gravitate toward effective IT systems and standards. This provides a why, as well as financial incentive for the meaningful use of certified EHR technology to achieve health quality and efficiency goals such as reduction in errors, availability of real-time clinical information, alerts, clinical decision support, improvement in quality measures, and e-prescribing. Improvements to these items will be rewarded, while those facilities and providers not meeting these standards will have "payments adjusted" (if not met by 2015).[11]

LEARNING WHAT WORKS

As the American Organization of Nurse Executives has observed, "Integration of healthcare information technology is not an isolated implementation with a defined endpoint, but a continuous process of assessment, planning, implementation, and evaluation."[12]

The journey to ultra high-quality healthcare is a long-term campaign. If you're in it, you certainly want to be in it to win; why else proceed down such a path? It is key, therefore, to convey to C-level executives who want everything done "yesterday" the real-world time frame for projects of a large magnitude, the realistic results, and the value to the entire organization. Moreover, it's the *people* part of change management that makes the difference in converting a quality-conscious healthcare facility into an ultra-quality oriented healthcare facility—the type with a reputation that patients seek out far and wide.

When you're merely loading the software and manipulating the project variables, you can only take your project so far. If you don't transform the people in the process, you'll forever be wondering why you can't accomplish your objectives.

People First, System Second

You might be predisposed to believe that raising healthcare quality across the board is a three-, six-, or nine-month project, or that setting a go-live date that everybody aims for will suffice to launch implementation and that, at that deadline, everything will be fine. It doesn't all start next Tuesday and proceed for the next couple of weeks until everyone gets the kinks out. This is an antiquated mindset that seeks to design a system and then plug people into it. Actually, the opposite is much closer to the reality of effectively implementing major organizational changes.

If you are the chief executive officer (CEO) or someone who happens to be data-driven, it's time to gain an understanding of the importance of the *people* side of the equation. This isn't innate in data-driven types who, by nature, are heavily left-brained, logical, and rational. Reports, charts, and graphs are their domain. They wish that plans were expertly implemented and that all one has to do is flip a switch and everything will work on the first pass.

Financial officers face slightly different but equally challenging hurdles. They say, "Why should I spend money investing in the people part of transformation? Can't we simply tell people what to do?" And then there are the chief operating officers (COOs) who acknowledge they have a business to run but don't want to upset the positions and job descriptions of the people they have put into place. They simply want to get things done.

Chief medical officers (CMO) moan that yes, they've got to care for patients, but they also have to ensure that their physicians are well-represented, while chief nursing officers (CNOs) lament, "My nurses are from an older generation. They don't understand computers. This isn't going to help them. The organization has already asked them to take on too much change. This is merely another set of burdensome obligations, and they are already way too busy."

Every chief officer of every division has a ready-made set of excuses and, amazingly, most of them are valid. Current operations, however, don't result in ensuring the higher quality patient care that is mandatory for healthcare today. What's more, book after book, from the 1980s to the present, has outlined in detail the importance of alignment—having everybody hum the same tune, or "teaching the elephant to dance."

The larger the organization, the more difficult it is to instill transformation. Having people state the founder's vision or even a one-sentence mantra about the vision is difficult to do, let alone inducing them to adopt a new set of behaviors.

THE WISDOM OF "SYSTEMNESS"

Many multi-facility hospital systems that otherwise have a high-quality reputation grapple with bringing each of their facilities into alignment. Each facility does something slightly different than the others, with no cohesion. Yet, consumers crave intra-facility consistency and *systemness*.

Consider your local supermarket and how it's laid out. In Florida, Publix Supermarkets offer a consistent shopping experience: turn to the right for vegetables and fruits. Go all the way to the back to find milk and cheese. Items will largely be in the same places in store after store.

If you visit a healthcare system that hasn't made a commitment to systemness, expect wide variations in patients' experiences and in quality of care. Significant variation translates to poor quality.

In one early project meeting, emergency department (ED) physicians and nurses were gathered from across multiple acute care facilities. Each operated differently. Whether it was caring for a patient experiencing chest pain or a stroke victim, each had its own protocols and set of standards. Like the scene in the movie *Apollo 13* where the flight crew in space had to join a round connector and a square connector, the operational procedures in the various EDs did not align with one another.

At the meeting, participants discussed how they handled particular procedures. "Oh, you do it that way? We didn't know. We've been doing it this way." They interacted with one another and slowly came to agreement and consensus as to the best ways to deliver care. It wasn't easy. At first, the variation was so wide that no one could get a handle on it at all.

The meeting chair recognized three distinct patterns of operation. He told each group to go to a corner and list their procedures for handling chest pain, etc. He then reassembled the three groups and compared their procedures. And actually, nearly 97 percent of the approaches taken by these three different groups were the same.

When the minor three percent difference from group to group was emphasized, the chairperson was able to enlist the cooperation of everyone in attendance. They thought to themselves, "We can agree on three percent. We can manage this." Likewise, in your own facility or organization, seemingly unending variation exists among departments, yet often you can find sufficient similarities in procedure to induce group-wide buy-in.

A Predictable Experience

Often, the variations in procedures are minor but are not recognized as such. Suppose one group starts with one or two preliminary but not necessarily crucial steps. If another group skips these steps and starts with "step 3," that puts the two groups out of sync. When they understand their difference, i.e., one has two preliminary non-critical steps, they can achieve resolution more quickly.

One reason the ghastly events of September 11, 2001 happened is that federal agencies weren't communicating with one another. By legislation, mandate, or bureaucratic procedure, one agency dispensed one kind of protection, while another agency dispensed something else; they lacked systemness. They were unable to compare notes and say, "These individuals are taking flying lessons, but have no interest in landing a plane."

Many individuals equate the term *system* to "how we do things here," as if restrictions abound. When a good system is in place, however, the consumer has a predictable—and hopefully positive—experience.

A well-designed system facilitates a level of comfort for all parties who can rely on the fact that when they turn right, they'll encounter this, and when they turn left, they'll encounter that. Within a healthcare facility, a good system allows for creativity and variation when merited. The overall system, however, still remains intact. The patient has a good idea of how things operate because you've taken the time to ensure that all system elements are in place.

TRANSFORMATION CAMPAIGNS AND ETERNITY

Some people have an uneasy time grappling with the reality that an effective transformation campaign goes on forever. Effective change is a series of interactions that result in *campaigns that go on with no ending point.*

Planned, intentional transformation needs to start on the frontline, engaging everyone with top management's vision. Effective change requires being involved with frontline staff daily, explaining what's in the transformation for them, how the changes will impact real-world quality of care, and how they can succeed. It requires providing them with support and incentives to do the right things over and over again. It's amazing how many organizations attempt to implement change without fully involving their frontline staff.

The biggest challenges that your hospital is likely to face include developing and implementing a patient care process enabled by IT that *has everyone involved.* This involves ensuring that top leadership can communicate the vision and provide steadfast support during this ongoing journey. It's not a sprint; it's a marathon, and the finish line is far out in the future.

If you are serving as the change agent, you'll need buy-in from all the C-level executives as well as all the troops who will be involved in the process. Otherwise, grappling with such a transition will represent an intellectually frustrating exercise. The chairman, president, or CEO must understand that the transformation campaign becomes part and parcel of everything he or she says or does from now on.

INSIGHTS AND LESSONS LEARNED

- Healthcare practitioners need to establish a new foundation that results in better, more reliable, and more responsive care because no higher calling exists among hospitals than to take good and safe care of patients.
- Evidence-based medicine can be harnessed through systems that allow you to leverage your data and transform them into information and knowlege by drawing upon the best of what else is known to truly work, and then apply this knowledge in a variety of settings.
- If you are a data-driven individual, it's time to embrace the *people* side of transformation: no campaign can succeed without winning over the people who must implement and live with the transformation.

- Healthcare consumers seek predictable high-quality experiences, which systemness can provide.
- As a change agent, you need buy-in from all the C-level executives and all role players who will be involved in the transformation process; otherwise, expect frustration.

THINKING FORWARD

1. Who is the champion or change agent to shepherd the development of your EHR implementation program? Are the right resources available to this individual?
2. Do you have a defined transformation management program in place?
3. Is a systemness focus part of your strategic and program plans?
4. What is your overall business strategy for harnessing the power of data and transforming it into actionable knowledge?

REFERENCES

1. H.R. 1–2. American Recovery and Reinvestment Act. Title XIII. Sec. 13001. Health Information Technology for Economic and Clinical Health Act (2009).

2. Blumenthal D, Tavenner M. The *Meaningful Use* regulation for electronic health records. *N Engl J Med* 2010; 363(6):501-504.

3. H.R. 3590, Patient Protection and Affordable Care Act of 2010.

4. Institute of Medicine, Committee on Quality of Health Care in America. Errors in Healthcare. A Leading Cause of Death and Injury. In: *To Err Is Human*. Washington, DC: National Academies Press; 2000: 26-48.

5. Institute of Medicine. *Crossing the Quality Chasm: A New Health System for the 21st Century*. Washington, DC: National Academies Press; 2001.

6. Klevens RM, Edwards JR, Richards CL Jr, et al. Estimating health care-associated infections and deaths in U.S. hospitals, 2002. *Public Health Report* 2007; 122(2):160-166.

7. Eber MR, Laxminarayan R, Perencevich EN, et al. Clinical and economic outcomes attributable to health care–associated sepsis and pneumonia. *Arch Intern Med* 2010; 170(4):347-353.

8. Frankovich J, Longhurst C, Sutherland S. Evidence-based medicine in the EHR era. *N Engl J Med* 2011; 365(19):1758-1759.

9. U.S. National Library of Medicine. Unified Medical Language System. UMLS Quick Start Guide. Available at www.nlm.nih.gov/research/umls/quickstart.html#What_is_the_UMLS. Accessed September 9, 2011.

10. HIMSS Analytics. 2012. U.S. EMR Adoption Model.^{SM} Available at www.himssanalytics.org/stagesGraph.asp. Accessed January 21, 2012.

11. Centers for Medicare & Medicaid Services. 2011. EHR Incentive Program Overview. Available at www.cms.gov/EHRIncentivePrograms/. Acessed January 22, 2012.

12. American Organization for Nurse Executives. AONE Toolkit for the nurse executive in the acquisition and implementation of information systems. p. 2. Available at www.aone.org. Accessed September 10, 2011.

CHAPTER 2

Setting the Stage for a Successful EHR Implementation

INTRODUCTION

The past 20 years have witnessed the formation of large regionalized healthcare delivery systems (e.g., integrated delivery networks, physician hospital organizations, multi-specialty group practices, etc.). The objectives of these systems are to reduce costs, share best practices, and strengthen each facility's share of the local market. This quest has been driven by growing technological capabilities as well as the desire to reduce errors while increasing profitability.

Part of the impetus in establishing large integrated health systems is to develop a coordinated approach to provide patient care efficiently and effectively with the patient as the center of focus. A common EHR is a key enabler to making this happen.

The value of cross-communication between hospitals, physician offices, and other care delivery sites is clear; change agents, therefore, must enlist the entire organizational structure—all medical professionals, administrators, staff, patients, and the larger community—to create a meaningful vision for the future. A clinical and organizational transformation initiative needs to fully engage the culture for years to come. Nothing short of that will markedly improve the quality of patient care far into the future.

Acknowledging where you are and what you already have is essential to any transformation. No organization exists in a vacuum or has an ideal platform. Transformation agents need to work within the current state of the organization's culture.

CREATING A VISION FOR THE FUTURE

Anyone in your organization who has the notion that getting an EHR up and running is simply a matter of buying the right platform or software and that this can be accomplished in a couple of months is setting themself up to fail. Properly implementing this type of project is not about technology; it's about inducing people to participate and accept change. All other project elements need to be in place, but people are the drivers. Without their buy-in, all the plans in the world are merely plans, which end up sitting on shelves. The project's role players and stakeholders have to embrace the project on many levels, and ultimately have it in their hearts.

Managing complex change, as noted in the book *Creating an Inclusive School*,[1] requires having the vision, skills, incentives, proper resources, and an action plan in place.

- If you are devoid of a sustaining vision, you end up with misdirection and confusion.
- If you fail to offer the right incentives, people exhibit the wrong kinds of behavior.
- If you are short on resources, frustration rises while milestones are compromised.
- If you are operating without an action plan then, realistically, how can you proceed even another day?

Organizational transformation is the key to offering high-quality care to each patient, one at a time. But it represents a continual process and not just an event. To begin the process, the CEO and senior leadership must target the entire healthcare team, from top to bottom, across all facilities, with messaging that drives delivery of superior patient-centered care. They must recognize that it is necessary to maintain and update the comprehensive medical information that is part and parcel to such care. This support must be clear and visible.

Many hospitals experience rapid growth but lack the ability to share real-time clinical information, in part because organizations are resistant to needed changes.

When employing a process-improvement approach, it is critical that your CEO and senior leaders agree on several foundational principles. They must recognize that this is not an IT project but a transformation initiative. Without this high-level support and participation, frontline staff will interpret such initiatives as just another "flavor of the month" and not embrace the work required for transformation.

Examining the current state of key processes in all departments in different ways leads to the identification of opportunities for improvement that should be embedded in the design of the future state operations, along with policies and procedures to help set the foundation for adoption. By taking governance-approved workflows to each hospital or department prior to a go-live and reviewing them with local stakeholders and leadership, opportunities, variations, and policy changes can be identified and managed. This process is further discussed in Chapter 4.

Any hospital or facility in a system, left on its own, will develop its own ways of proceeding which may not always be evidence-based. There is a tendency to continue to do what has always been done, versus striving toward changing and standardizing practice based on evidence. Despite a vast volume of published evidence, implementing evidence-based practice is challenging and requires a paradigm shift and cultural change within an organization.[2]

To achieve smoother operations, greater profitability, and regional prominence, all facilities must practice to the same standard required of all other facilities in a healthcare system. By sharing knowledge between facilities, everyone employed by or served by a health system stands to gain.

MANAGING EXPECTATIONS

Many healthcare systems lack the requisite vision, resources, or knowledge of the leadership requirements needed to initiate and succeed in a large-scale implementation project. To prepare an organization to work through an implementation process, the key first steps are agreeing to a time-line, process, and budget. The notion of practicing to a standard is key.

Often, clinical leadership and other departments have little knowledge about the steps involved in making a systemwide transformation project a reality. Organizations that are planning to install an EHR are likely to encounter pushback when asking people to change how they do their work. This is especially true in the early stages of adopting EHRs when few users and leaders have knowledge and experience in the use of online clinical information technology. Expectations can be managed by educating users and leadership about the impending changes and what it means to them, showing them the benefits and leveraging governance to manage variations.

To gain support from the frontline users, their participation must be secured and they must be engaged in the planning and system selection process. Clinicians and physicians have established patterns in the ways they practice medicine and deliver bedside care. They expect that any change will require more work and take more time. They must be educated about the impact of learning new processes and the impact of these on productivity. Project leaders must be transparent about the amount of work needed to implement change and transition to an EHR-driven environment of care.

A multifaceted, advanced EHR quality initiative, which typically represents the most ambitious undertaking hospital systems have ever attempted, must be tied to key organizational strategic objectives and goals. It must be aligned with key principles such as timely access to patient information and increased quality and patient safety.

Such projects must strive to ensure that treatments are given more accurately, decisions are made more quickly and effectively, and diagnoses are more precise because of timely access to clinical information. Ultimately, information can be shared more easily with patients, who have a right to their own records.

As a result, physicians within a hospital and from any location will be able to access and communicate patient information across the healthcare delivery system in real time. All others who need patient information are able to access it more quickly and easily as well. Systemwide, practicing to a standard is consistent with a commitment to quality and offers a means of collaboration among professional staff and between facilities.

A PHASED APPROACH VERSUS BIG BANG

Healthcare information is the key enabler for effective healthcare transformation. Choosing which approach to use, whether it's phased or big bang, is a critical organizational transformation decision. There are pros and cons to each, and the approach needs to align with your organizational culture and tolerance for change.

One option is a phased approach, which is often chosen to reduce overall adoption risk and brings certain parts of the organization live with various system applications to establish specific functionalities in a planned sequential manner. This approach allows a health system's end users to adapt over time to a culture of electronic documentation and practicing to a standard. One example of a phased approach is outlined next:

Phase 1: Clinical Core – This initial phase involves implementation of the EHR system within health information management, surgery, and pharmacy departments and adding nursing and ancillary documentation, computer provider order entry (CPOE) and other physician documentation in focused areas such as the emergency departments and electronic medication administration records (eMARs).

Phase 2: Outcomes Optimization – The second phase involves implementation of hospital-wide inpatient CPOE and structured physician documentation, anesthesia documentation and/or some of the other more challenging areas such as maternity, clinical decision support (e.g., alerts, rules, etc.), bar-coded medication administration, and quality reporting.

When planning to implement inpatient CPOE, it is key to implement this in a later phase. This decision ensures that the organization will have in place the best support and complementary technologies to optimize efficiency for physicians when completing electronic documentation and order entry.

Progression toward implementing full functionality of an EHR is vital, but equally so is helping people move effectively through a major transformation process. The phased approach, combined with a change management methodology, is fundamental in helping an organization ease into an EHR-driven environment.

A second option is a big bang approach, which brings up all applications and functionality at one time. This allows for a quicker migration to new workflows and decreases the hybrid paper and computer state. It also increases the amount of stress on the clinican team as they transition to a new world. It is key to have strong executive leadership for this approach as well.

Note that there is no right or wrong approach to implementation. It is really dependent on your organization's tolerance for change, as well as available resources and funding.

WHAT TRANSFORMATION MODEL TO EMPLOY

When putting your stake in the ground, use an established change model to serve as a guidepost. One such model is the methodology described by Professor John Kotter of Harvard University. Kotter is heir to a long and proud tradition of doctoral level instructors, management consultants, and change management experts whose methods rose in popularity following World War II (see Appendix A.).

Kotter co-authored the book *Our Iceberg Is Melting*, a quick and easy read, but also a deceptively powerful guide for transformation agents. Kotter's methodology[3] for transformation encompasses three basic areas, each of which has sub-steps as described in Figure 2-1.

1. The first basic area of focus, termed "Prepare," involves setting the stage and deciding what to accomplish. The mission here is to create a sense of urgency, assemble the team, and develop the transformation vision and strategy.

2. The second basic area, termed "Engage," focuses on making things happen and includes communicating with all role players and stakeholders to gain their buy-in, empowering and enabling others to take appropriate actions in support of the project objectives, and creating short-term wins.

3. Once the transformation has occurred, do not let up on the path to establishing a new culture. The third stage, termed "Sustain," is all

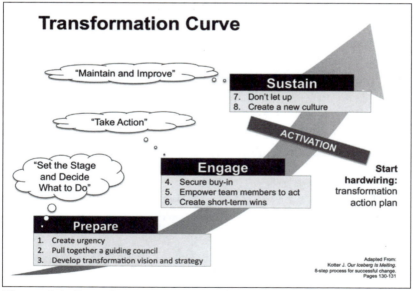

Figure 2-1: Transformation Model for EHR and ACO Adoption

about making the new processes stick and involves creating a new culture, evaluating progress and communicating this progress to the organization to ensure transparency of the results of everyone's effort.

DELIVERING THE NEWS: CREATE A SENSE OF URGENCY

In the first stage of the transformation model, *set the stage and decide what to do*. Top leaders must communicate to all concerned that a big transition is coming and they should prepare for it—and do so with a sense of urgency. Before deciding how and when to communicate, survey senior and mid-level management to discover how open they are to doing things differently and their estimation of the level of collaboration in the organization.

Quickly, after establishing this sense of urgency, survey every single employee in your organization with the same kinds of questions. Once you have all the data in hand, use them to help your hospital's CEO craft a message that will have optimal impact. Top executives who report to the CEO should employ all manner of communication—speeches, emails, memos, videos, even Facebook and Twitter, if it fits the culture—to get the word out in various forms and reinforce these types of messages:

- Our organization is going to move from point A to point B, and we will never be the same.
- We will never return to the past; we are committed to creating a different kind of future.
- You play an important role in this transformation.
- We are counting on your participation and dedication.
- This is not a finite project with a clear ending point.
- This will be an everlasting transformation for our culture.
- This transformation will continually require modifications and refinements.
- Training and support will be in place to help you make this transition.

Develop videos with CEOs and other top executives delivering these messages, and make them available for each employee in your organization to view. This is a huge undertaking, but well worth it. Employees directly receive the message that this quality initiative is critical to future success and supporting it is their primary objective each day.

When employees, especially those who have never been exposed to a similar project, receive a video recording from their CEO they sense that a fundamental shift in operations is at hand. This messaging cannot be overemphasized, as it sets the tone and begins the transformation process. Consider hiring a communications expert to help you with this work.

ESTABLISHING A GUIDING TEAM

Assemble a team composed of people who understand the clinical side of operations. This transformation initiative should not be launched as an IT project. In reverse of what often occurs in major initiatives, technology should result from clinical transformation, not vice versa. Clinically driven projects must focus on clinical workflows, quality improvement, and patient safety. Keep such factors in mind when selecting members of the project team, which must include clinicians.

Create new job descriptions and hire analysts with a clinical background, versus those with strictly IT skills, so that the employees building the EHR tools are the same employees using them. It may be easier to hire nurses and pharmacists and teach them IT skills than to hire individuals with IT backgrounds but no clinical skills.

Key stakeholder participation is needed throughout the process. An organization should establish clinical ownership at the lowest level by clearly defining the vision, goals, and expected involvement of every individual involved in the large transformation effort.

Ensure the guiding team consists of leaders who have long been with the organization and command high levels of respect and trust. In one organization, one of the guiding team members was a chief nursing officer (CNO) who had been with the organization for more than 20 years and was extremely well-regarded by her colleagues. At first she wasn't thrilled about being on the guiding team, but she worried that if she didn't get involved things would go awry. Over time, she became committed to the EHR project and was gratified that she played such a key role.

Executives who hold responsibility for interacting with physicians need strong leadership support and knowledge of EHRs. They need all executive level staff to encourage physician adoption of the EHR.

Does being a member of the guiding team (or other groups to be discussed) add to employees' work hours per week? Do they have to fit in their participation with what they're already doing? The answer is yes. It adds tremendously to their workload. However, in the long run, they will see that the benefits far outweigh the extra effort they expend. They may not think so at first, but in time they will find it to be true. An element of prestige accrues to high-ranking team contributors that is difficult to describe but is nonetheless rewarding.

While the guiding team receives no extra pay, they experience a sense of reward as they witness how plans they put into place are being implemented, how an entire culture has transformed, and how the community has responded. Remember that a transformation initiative of this size should be decreed by the CEO as the organization's most important project.

Defining the Time Frame

It's one thing to outline the forthcoming transformation, establish the vision, and develop the strategy; it's quite another to decide how much time and effort to expend. Is it a 12-month project? Is it a three-year project? At the outset, it's difficult to know without careful planning.

Top executives debate this issue extensively. Some say a transformation of this magnitude in 12 or even 24 months would be too much, too fast. They may reason that taking a quicker, less expensive path would likely result in less efficiency, weaker adoption, and failure to meet project goals. They may fear disruption and high resistance. After mulling over the issue, a guiding team might determine that an initiative would extend for five years or longer. Most organizations don't make that level of commitment, but it all depends on each organization's culture.

DEVELOP THE VISION

Once you have committed time and money, it should be clear to everyone that the organization's transformation is inevitable. At this point, you should settle on an effective project vision. One example might be: "This project will enable our entire healthcare team to deliver top quality patient-centered care by providing comprehensive information at the right place at the right time." You must then elaborate on the many ways that the EHR project would benefit patients, such as:

- Diagnosis will be more precise, with access to all of a patient's medical data and longitudinal information.
- Treatments will be more accurate.
- Healthcare professionals will be able to spend more time at their patients' bedsides.
- Decisions will be made more quickly and more effectively.
- Information will be more easily and readily shared with patients.

ENGAGE: TAKE ACTION

The second stage in the transformation model is to "take action" and includes three basic activities: communicate for buy-in, empower and enable others to act, and create short-term wins.

To communicate for buy-in, assemble the principal members of the project team to develop a series of key messages. Brainstorm together, post charts on the wall, modify and combine ideas, and perhaps drop some ideas altogether. Recognize the need early in a project's life cycle to develop a series of unique messages for the various constituencies. All told, you may develop hundreds of messages to be dispensed over several years, averaging around 50 messages annually, depending on the size of your project.

Retain an advertising agency to help devise effective messages. For example, you may tell the agency you need to improve patient safety in your organization. The agency representatives would then walk you through what that means for physicians, for employees, and for patients. Because communication is so critical, hire a communications specialist to serve on the project team. This is an unusual move in most organizations, but communication is essential to the transformation initiative and such resources are necessary.

Compensation for Dislocation

To send the message that you are serious about engaging all staff members in an organization, allocate funds to secure bedside clinician participation. Designate them as subject matter experts for the project, and pay their respective departments for the time spent helping on the project instead of caring for patients.

Consider employees who work 40-hour weeks. If you need them fully engaged in the project, pull them away from patients' bedsides altogether so they can provide their insights and knowledge. Their compensation should come out of the project budget, not their respective departments' budgets.

Paying frontline people from the project budget enables you to receive valuable input from them. They understand best how their roles need to transform at the department and staff levels. Otherwise, you might be sending a message that the project team is making all the decisions or simply dispensing change management "claptrap."

Enabling Others to Act

As an example, at one large hospital there were approximately 250 frontline employees who were considered subject matter experts and were responsble for guiding the detailed design decision-making process. The parts of the system that impacted employees were designed by those employees. The parts of the system that impacted physicians were designed by those physicians, and so on. Employ a process in which you create a decision-making matrix detailing what decisions will be made at each level in the organization, as depicted in Table 2-1.

As project leaders, you will *not* make some decisions, as surprising as that might sound. Frontline people will. Your role is to help drive consensus, but no more. The CNO sat at the helm and conducted gov-

Organization	RN	Pharmacist	RT	Physician
Who suspends medications		X		
Who enters orders	X			X
Who documents pain scores	X			
Who enters oxygen measures			X	

Table 2-1: Decision-Making Matrix

ernance meetings to address the disagreements among participants concerning implementation of the new system. An EHR is owned by the staff that designed it, not the project team.

CREATING SHORT-TERM WINS

The third element of "take action" is creating short-term wins. It's easier for an organization to accept broad, sweeping transformation if those impacted can discern that there is something in it for them.

A short-term win, for example, might be the ability to house all clinical results (such as lab results) in one place that can be easily accessed by clinicians. In contrast, clinicians formerly may have had to spend hours hunting down a chart on the floor. Sometimes the paper charts traveled easily; too often they did not. If one of the clinicians happened to pick up a chart and leave it down the hall, another clinician may have wasted 10–15 minutes tracking down that chart.

Once you establish an EHR foundation and go "live" with it, members of the healthcare delivery team can access patient information from any place—including another floor, another hospital, at home, or while traveling. If someone needs to make a change to the record, an electronic stamping system and signature process registers the change and makes it transparent to all other users.

The short term win, the "what's in it for me" in this example, was that clinicians would have easier access to information. That might not sound like a great benefit, but when you consider how much easier and more efficient that makes a healthcare professional's life, it's a huge transformation.

In one organiztion, two nurses came running down the hall in a panic as the EHR Director was sitting in a Go-Live Command Center. They said frantically, "We have a patient who just came from the emergency room, and we have no information on him. We have no clue what to do!"

The EHR Director said, "All you have to do is sign in, type the patient's name, and you can see his chart, including all that happened in the ED, and all of his test results. You can see what equipment to have ready and be totally prepared for the patient's arrival." The nurses were pleasantly surprised. One of them said, "I can do that from my floor, even though the patient has barely left the ED?" The EHR Director offered her a resounding, "Yes. Welcome to the EHR!"

Navigating on the First Try

Physicians, nurses, and other clinicians who need to access real-time, up-to-date information quickly discover that logging into the EHR system is actually easy. They can navigate their way virtually on first use and instead of relying on "chicken-scrawl-type" handwriting on a piece of paper, they are treated to clear, on-screen text.

For physicians, the "what's in it for me" question is also easily answered. At midnight while making the rounds, or even from home, they might need to call and receive an update on a patient. Often, they are put on hold while a nurse searches for the chart. Or, if lab results weren't printed, the physicians would have to call the lab.

As elements of the EHR become available, if a physician needs a patient update or is paged directly by the nurse, the physician can log in and view the chart and real-time details of the patient's situation from home or the office instead of having to call around and interrupt people who are often equally frustrated.

Management sage Peter Drucker, PhD, observed that for a system-wide transformation to be embraced, it must be perceived as offering ten times the advantages over the old way.[4] With this in mind, offer targets of transformation: rapid, short-term wins that are ultra-easy to implement and yield immediate benefits.

SUSTAIN, MAINTAIN, AND IMPROVE

Sustaining the transformation is the third stage of the transformation model. *Stickiness*, a term gaining favor in recent years, is vital to ensure that operations don't slip back to old, familiar ways.

Consider the following example from one organization: Soon after a project was initiated, the team discovered that the surgical department in one of its hospitals sought to revert back to a paper-based documentation system. Department heads claimed that charting and documenting patients' progress was taking too long, surgeries were becoming backed up, and the new system was unreliable.

At the time, the department was five days into the new process, still ascending the learning curve. "We've made the decision for ourselves not to employ the new system," they reported, "and to return to the paper system, which worked quite well for us." The chief information officer's (CIO's) response was to immediately go to the hospital and meet with those involved. Once the surgical unit managers and leadership team were seated around the table, the CIO told them, "The decision isn't one you can make on your own. We make all decisions as a group. Now, what are the issues?"

The managers raised a litany of issues, many of them valid and reasonable. So, a team was posted on site to guide the surgical staff through every twist and turn with a committment to bringing them into the fold and having everything work out. The support group assembled for the surgical unit consisted of clinical IT analysts as well as employees who had worked on the project team and were highly skilled in the knowledge of both surgical workflow and the design of the system.

One of the team members observed that the surgical nurses were documenting every single field that the software contained—scores and scores of items—instead of only the five or six critical items that merited attention. In other words, they were quickly falling behind, filling in unnecessary fields with responses such as *yes, no,* or *not applicable.* The on-site team worked with them, explaining how to employ the system for optimal gain and discouraging anyone from reverting to old ways.

The CIO's prompt action in this example was impressive. He had assembled people from other departments and reallocated them to the surgical department. The CIO might have sought to phone in a solution, send a representative, or take other action that would have been less effective in the long run. It's true that the other departments from which members of the support team had been extricated now had fewer people for two weeks. But those pulled off their regular assignments knew that it was part of their job.

Within two weeks, an "Aha!" moment occurred for the surgical department. The staff started to become adept at filling in the documentation online and arrived at the point where they thought they could handle it themselves. Whereas earlier they were in panic mode and willing to scrap the entire system, they now conceded that it worked well and provided an array of benefits they hadn't understood before.

In gathering their feedback, the project team also went back to the drawing board and helped to devise a simpler form. They learned that they had probably overbuilt some elements of the system. They understood from their experience that they had to maintain flexibility. As in Janelle Barlow and Claus Moller's book, *A Complaint is a Gift,*[5] they came to realize that the problem they experienced helped them to improve the system and, thus, likely helped to decrease resistance from other departments at other facilities.

Surgical teams were involved in the original design of the system, including participants from this particular hospital. They thought they didn't have any part in the system design. In truth, they must have simply forgotten they had participated. They probably hadn't fully realized the ramifications at the time they were engaged in the design of the system. Understandably, they had to actually work with the system to gain a fuller view.

This example illustrates that exhibiting a "don't let up" posture is necessary; otherwise, all of your prior progress on the project can come undone. Allowing one department in one facility to secede could have had a ripple effect, like Abraham Lincoln telling only Georgia, "Okay, you can secede."

CREATING A NEW CULTURE

Introducing a new system is not a one-time event. Your project team must constantly examine the various facilities and departments and monitor who's making satisfactory progress and who's having problems.

Periodic reinforcement is required to create a new culture, the second element of "maintain and improve." This can take months or longer. You must vigilantly monitor progress, often behind the scenes. Having super users in place (see Chapter 4) who are the on-site guides, one-on-one coaches, and advocates of the system to whom others can readily turn for support is key to success.

Reinforcement takes many forms. At one facility, a group of respiratory therapists couldn't agree on using the standard set of system tools. They were at odds about how to design the system. They didn't see how they were going to benefit from the system, and many doubted its value.

They met in a conference room with the system's CNO, chief operating officers (COOs), and directors of respiratory therapy. One director presented a strong case for why the respiratory therapists did not want to adopt the new system. They were already using a highly customized stand-alone system that had met every single one of their needs.

It became apparent at the first meeting, which got pretty heated at times, that other meetings would be needed to drive consensus. At each meeting, the leadership team reinforced "what was in it" for the respiratory therapists as well as operational leaders. Eventually, over a period of a few months, the methodology worked; for the first time ever, the respiratory therapists from across the health system formed a collaborative group and worked together in designing the new tools and standards of practice.

Planning and implementing an EHR requires a great deal of patience. Many days, tough choices need to be made. Not everyone will be in agreement. Pockets of resistance will emerge. You have to keep explaining, coaching, guiding and listening, and touting the benefits. Strive to guide stakeholders in a way that leaves everyone feeling good about the interaction. Help the teams to understand that the new system will provide the patient with a better experience and an improved level of care. In the previous example, this is what eventually brought the respiratory therapists on board. Once they began working in unison, they understood the full measure of the benefits now available to them. Everyone involved was committed, and no one would turn back. A new culture had taken hold.

The respiratory therapists' achievement was a breakthrough for this organzation. Perhaps every other time they had been confronted by some transformation initiative or a change agent walked through their door, they silently winced, experienced an energy drop, and thought to themselves, "Here we go again." Like others, the respiratory therapists had probably heard before, "This is all about helping the patient."

The difference this time was that they had the opportunity to exercise control over how the new system would affect their department— and that the COOs had sat down with them and conveyed that they were committed to making this transformation initiative work.

Creating the Win-Win

To create the win-win scenario, it pays to be able to "wear the hat" or "walk in the moccasins" of the other party. In one organization, a CNO was contemplating entering respiratory data in one system and other clinical data in a separate, homegrown system. The EHR director, who had been a neonatal intensive care unit (NICU) nurse for a long time, put on her NICU hat. She knew that the CNO was committed to taking care of her nurses. Yet, she also knew that many premature babies have respiratory problems, and it's difficult for the nurse as well as the physician to provide quality care if respiratory data are in a separate system. Why not enable them to take better care of their patients?

The NICU explained how, with the new technology, the data the nurses needed would be available in the EHR right from their monitors. So, the nurses wouldn't be looking around, writing things down multiple times, and eating up valuable time. In general, nurses love that kind of data integration because it saves them time. The NICU emphasized that point with the CNO and could see her contemplating the change.

If creating a new culture were easy, you could snap your fingers and have it be so. Software can be perfected, the system can be refined, but the human dynamic of transformation is the most challenging.

OVERSIGHT BOARDS AND VENDORS

Focused involvement plus sponsorship by a senior leadership team working in cooperation with system vendors results in strong, system-wide support. That's one kind of partnership. Develop an executive oversight board that convenes on a regular basis to facilitate the governance of the key activities.

An executive oversight board, which should include your system's senior leadership as well as the software vendor's senior leadership, discusses strategic issues and provides oversight for a project. The board deals with clinical adoption of new technology, high-level program review, performance metrics, vendor and client collaboration, and addresses any challenges that require executive level attention to ensure resolution.

At one organization, an unexpected software downtime occurred in the midst of a large upgrade. The vendor took nearly eight hours to get the organization back up and running. When you're dependent on electronic technology to treat patients, eight hours seems like a lifetime. Fortunately, the next executive oversight meeting was several weeks away, which gave everyone time to gain their composure.

At the meeting, the CEO expressed his extreme dissatisfaction to the vendor's senior leaders. Unquestionably, the vendor was concerned for more than merely obvious reasons: this organization had a risk-and-reward relationship with the vendor. Part of the annual revenue was based upon achieving a particular level of customer satisfaction. This is how it works:

Everyone from frontline clinicians to managers of the department in which the EHR tools are being implemented provides feedback on the effectiveness of the system. Have them provide monthly feedback via a vote and tie the payment model to that vote, which will determine how much revenue the vendor will receive.

When the vendor hasn't met the requisite scores, the vendor should receive less than full payment. Focus on milestones achieved rather than hours expended by the vendor or line item services provided by a certain date. EHR projects are flawed at the outset when they're based on project due dates. Chasing the goal of having the system be "on" by a particular date invariably causes misalignments and less-than-desirable outcomes. Not all vendors are willing to proceed based on milestones achieved, so you have to choose vendors carefully and negotiate.

RISK AND REWARD FOR VENDORS

Payments to vendors should not be based merely on milestones or system updates. The quality of patient care and level of service are key factors as well. The agreement with the vendor should extend to quality measures such as decreasing patient falls, reducing the number of pressure ulcers, and decreasing infections. Sit down with your clinical leadership prior to signing a vendor contract and determine the most important quality initiatives for the organization where technology can be leveraged to help achieve them. Tie your vendor contract to achieving your organization-specific quality measures.

Most organizations don't negotiate with software vendors for those kinds of measures. As a result of implementing the right software and having the right tools and processes in place, however, you should expect falls, pressure ulcers, and infections to decrease. If they don't, the vendor receives less revenue.

Many organizations are especially interested in this last point. Some healthcare systems have employed risk and reward based on milestones, but not upon clinical outcomes.

How do you find vendors who are willing to proceed based on such criterion, and keep the relationship vibrant? These days, competitiveness alone will cause a vendor to say, "Yes, we can entertain that." Because of regulations and time constraints, choose a vendor with a solid reputation that has already designed software systems for many hospitals and larger health systems.

Even if you're a small hospital with limited funds, you want to strive to base your risk and reward relationship with your vendor on clinical outcomes. That is the only way to guarantee that you will unmistakably achieve significant, long-term, desirable transformation and improved outcomes. Also, if you're part of a smaller health system, you have options when it comes to choosing vendors. Many vendors are willing to demonstrate what they can do for you and to partner with you if it results in a long-term stream of revenues. Find a vendor with an off-the-shelf system that's close to what you want.

As healthcare providers our competency isn't software development, and we don't have the ability to develop the source code. Our competency is healthcare and empowering the people that make it work.

INSIGHTS AND LESSONS LEARNED

- Change agents need to work with the culture as it is and be aware of people's predispositions to respond; no organization exists in a vacuum and acknowledging where you are and what you already have is essential to any transformation.
- A multifaceted quality initiative could represent the most ambitious undertaking your hospital system has ever attempted; it helps if top leadership communicates that to everyone.
- Progress toward full implementation and helping people move effectively through the transformation process are equally vital; thus, a multi-phased approach can be more advantageous than a big-bang approach.
- Employ a simple, effective transformation model to serve as your guidepost, perhaps one that can easily be understood from a single graphic.
- Many days, tough choices need to be made in implementing an EHR, and resistance will emerge; keep explaining, coaching, guiding and listening, and touting the benefits.
- Find a software vendor with a solid reputation and who is willing to partner and negotiate with you on tying your organization's quality measures to a vendor risk and reward model.

THINKING FORWARD

1. Do you have a transformation management model selected?
2. Have you selected a phased or big-bang approach for your EHR implementation?
3. Do you have a strong communications plan and resources to execute it?
4. Who is on your guiding team?

REFERENCES

1.   Falvey MA, Givnes CC. What is an inclusive school? In: Villa RA, Thousand JS, eds. *Creating an Inclusive School*. Alexandria, VA: Association for Supervision & Curriculum Development; 2005: 1-12.

2.   Kent B, Hutchinson A, Bioeth M, et al. Getting evidence into practice-understanding knowledge translation to achieve practice change. *Worldviews on Evidence-Based Nursing* 2009; 183-185.

3.   Kotter J, Rathgeber H. *Our Iceberg Is Melting*. New York: St. Martin's Press; 2005: 130-131.

4.   Drucker PF. *Managing In a Time of Great Change*. New York: Truman Talley Books/Plume; 1998; 145.

5.   Barlow J, Moller C. The customer speaks. *A Complaint is a Gift*. San Francisco, CA: Berrett-Koehler; 1996: 1-6.

CHAPTER 3

Foundations of Transformational Governance

INTRODUCTION

The success of any long-term transformation initiative depends on the degree to which those impacted by the organizational transformation not only participate in the process, but also *serve in a governing capacity*. In other words, they become owners as opposed to bystanders or casual participants.

To accomplish this, establish governance to involve more people in the process, distribute roles and responsibilities, lessen the burden on everyone concerned, and ensure that you have the right people at the right time in the right place to overcome challenges and make decisions as they unfold.

FORMING THE FOUNDATION

It is important to establish a governing structure that includes executive and clinical leadership from all stakeholder groups. All members of this governing structure should play a vital and distinct role in the project. The level of engagement that they are accorded demonstrates the organization's commitment to resolving conflict and handling multidisciplinary issues, whenever and wherever they arise throughout the system.

From the outset, executives need to invest considerable time, energy, and budgetary funds. Their role as leaders is to debate and decide on issues related to the selection, design, and implementation of the software that will convert the organization from silo operations to *systemness* driven by an EHR.

These executives then keep a keen eye on each phase of the project, ensuring that it meets both patient-centered and clinician-centric concerns. It is important for clinical leadership to own the design and construction of the system. Mirroring the executive leadership, they also have a huge per-person investment in success.

Part of establishing a governing structure involves the socialization of governing members: they need to meet, get to know each other, and form bonds. This is especially important as physicians play stronger leadership roles in healthcare delivery systems and as we move into the era of accountable care.

THREE TIERS OF GOVERNANCE

In any large-scale implementation, an organization needs to have an effective model for decision making in its governance model. One form of a governance model, as depicted in Figure 3-1, is based on three tiers. Each tier provides a structure for covering necessary decision making on a transformation project ranging from high-level strategic decisions to the detailed tactical and operational decisions required to ensure successful engagement of stakeholders and adoption of the new system, tools, or processes.

The first tier consists of high-level decisions, which have major significance throughout an organization. These decisions are handled by an Executive Project Oversight Committee that consists of the aforementioned executive and clinical leaders. At this level, questions asked include: "What will be done, and who will do it?" These are high-level decisions that generally represent less than 10 percent of all decisions made in conjunction with the implementation of the project.

The second tier consists of mid-level decisions, which represent perhaps 25 percent of all decisions related to a project. Decisions at this level have moderate impact throughout the organization and are the responsibility of a mid-level governance committee consisting of Clinical Directors from across the health system. Physician Advisory Councils, comprised of physician leadership from across the organization, also fall within this tier. They provide focused decision making in areas that primarily impact physicians. Mid-level decisions usually consist of answering the question, "How will something be done?" and

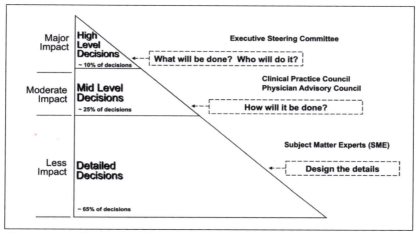

Figure 3-1: Three-Tier Governance Model

establishing new policy and procedures that will ensure the efficient workflow in redesigned health system operations.

The third level of decision making, regarded as detail decisions, accounts for the remaining 65 percent. They have less impact than mid-level or high-level decisions. Decisions at this level are the domain of the subject matter experts (SMEs), whose key concern is to address the myriad details that arise as a result of the key decisions made at the highest level. This framework provides clear guidelines and the basic foundational structure for decision making.

Decision Framework

At the start of a large-scale project, it is important to build the decision framework to support the foundation and the work of the teams. Gather all of the top executives throughout the healthcare system and present them with key decisions—those decisions necessary to launch the EHR implementation project requiring buy-in from the highest level stakeholders. Walk them through a patient-centered mini-case, which will help to answer many questions as to how the EHR might impact operations and workflow. Presenting a patient-centered story provides the executives with an understanding from the patient's eyes as to precisely what he or she will experience upon entering one of your hospitals.

A decision framework represents some notable and progressive measures. Examples of decisions might include the following:

- Hospitals will practice to a standard for clinical documentation and order entry.
- Hospitals will discontinue printing results.
- Hospitals will mandate electronic signatures by physicians for record completion.
- Hospitals will consider the electronic record the legal medical record.

You should lay out for your executives key decisions that will have to be in place for the rest of the team to be successful. Having them in one room to understand, discuss, and participate in these decisions offers an excellent shot-in-the-arm launch of an EHR implementation project.

DECISION POINTS

Decision points can prove to be an important element of the decision-making process. As you walk your executives through the patient-centered scenario, emphasize the following: "Here are the decision points that need to be reinforced. Here are the benefits, implications, cultural impacts, and costs of each step along this path." Also, rather than having EHR project leadership stand up before the group and present this mini-story, consider having members of your clinical leadership team drive this process, such as your CNO, CMO, and chief quality officer (CQO).

One idea to consider is to ask all of the executives to vote, by hand, as to whether or not they would support the decisions being discussed. They shouldn't leave the room until everyone has a hand raised and has affirmed their support. Then take a group photo and use it for reinforcement of the team's commitment in communications with employees.

In one organization, it was decided to tackle physician order entry in the emergency department before implementing house-wide CPOE. The project team proposed that physician order entry would be the standard in the emergency departments as the system's first point of conversion. Eventually, it would be the standard throughout all departments.

Upon hearing this, one of the CEOs wanted to know, "Why are you asking us merely to initiate physician order entry in the emergency

artments if ultimately it needs to be done everywhere? Let's make
decision now that it will be the standard across the health system."

Following her comment, participants eventually came to the con-
nsus that they could all support that decision. They raised their
ands and agreed. Thus, the first decision was: "Computerized physician order entry will be the standard."

ALL ABOUT BUY-IN

When you ask members of governance committees or other groups to
raise their hands in agreement, there should be little dissension. This
won't be because the value of the idea will be universally and immediately noteworthy. It will only happen if you begin speaking with them
long before they assemble. Starting at the C-level, months in advance,
visit each of the executives who will be in the committee room on the
day that voting will occur. Win them over one by one so that all of the
key executives remain in the loop, especially as you get closer to the
start of a new phase.

Each month, develop a set of talking points to help bring people
further along in the process. Anticipate questions that will be asked
and concerns that will be raised. Supply the talking points to leaders
throughout the organization who also have assumed responsibility
for ensuring long-term project success. These individiuals will be discussed in future chapters.

THE DECISION-MAKING LADDER

With three levels of governance corresponding to three levels of decision making, any issue regarded as a "detail" decision that didn't otherwise map to the basic framework should be routed up to the mid-level
governance group for its approval, and then routed up again to the
higher-level system governance group when needed. Figure 3-2 depicts
an example system of governance.

Every time an issue arises that has not previously been considered
or accounted for, it should be vetted by higher levels of governance.
This is very useful in ensuring that issues and concerns do not slip
through the cracks and that there is visibility and approval of the transformations being made through all levels in the organization.

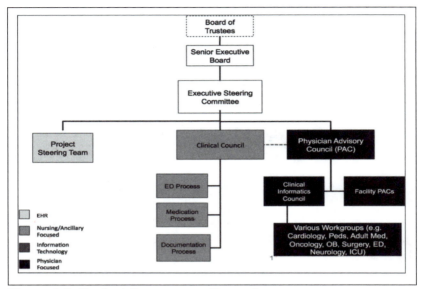

Figure 3-2: Project Governance Example

Challenges to Governance Decisions

Throughout the transformation process, one group after another will inevitably ask to have an exception made. They should be heard but invariably their requests will be denied. Initially, the ruling may sound like an edict to many people. Some may think, "The governing committee doesn't understand what we do. How can they be supportive of us? We're as passionate about providing good patient care as they are." Each time, the solution to this dilemma is effective communication about the benefits of the system and collaborative decision making.

Furthermore, the transformation team needs to maintain a united front and support needs to come from the top down. At one health system, for example, a group of cardiologists who were documenting in a stand-alone system requested an interface to the standard EHR so that their documentation and clinical data would flow to their system. The issue made its way up the governance chain to the highest group, where the clinicians presented their case. They said, "We think it's vital that the cardiologists are allowed this exception."

When the issue reached the CEO, his response was, "That request goes against the decisions we've made. We can't allow it." Like everyone else, the cardiology group would have to follow the process of entering and maintaining documentation in the standard EHR.

Later, the obstetric (OB) nurses at one of the hospitals questioned whether or not they had to document patient medications in the EHR. They argued that they were comfortable with the old system and that it worked well for them. After deliberation by the governance committee, they were told, "You must document medications in the new system. This is our standard, and it would not be safe to have medications in a separate system. It's not negotiable."

With the OB nurses, the governance group explained that having some elements of the patient's medical history outside of the system meant doing extra work. When the nurses understood that they could reduce steps and save time, they were won over. Concurrently, they still had an outlet for their views, as did all groups.

Any department in disagreement with any aspect of the system should be able to attend the next higher-level governance committee meeting and explain why they want to do things differently. Obviously, their rationale has to be convincing. Exceptions are quite rare, but sometimes a case can be made.

CASE STUDY:
USING A WELL-DEVELOPED GOVERNANCE STRUCTURE TO GUIDE DECISIONS

By Susan Heichert, BSN, MA, FHIMSS, Senior Vice President/Chief Information Officer, and Mary Lambert, MBA, RHIA, Director, Clinical Decision Support and Optimization, Allina Hospitals and Clinics, Minneapolis, Minnesota

INTRODUCTION

Allina Hospitals and Clinics provides healthcare services in Minnesota and Western Wisconsin, with the largest market share in the Twin Cities of Minneapolis and St. Paul. The system comprises 11 hospitals (~1,700 staffed beds), 82 clinics (both freestanding and hospital-based), and includes specialty operations including medical transportation, community pharmacies, lab outreach, home care, and hospice. Allina employs about 22,800 staff, including 1,200-plus employed physicians, primarily in the ambulatory division. Last year, Allina saw more than 109,000 inpatient admissions and more than 1 million outpatient visits.

The EHR journey began in 2003 when Allina determined to replace the mix of niche legacy system technology throughout the system with standard platforms for clinical and revenue cycle automation. Today there are more than 30,000 users of the EHR, 3 million patient records, and 240,000 patients who actively view health information, schedule appointments, pay bills, and conduct e-visits electronically. Additionally, Allina has extended the EHR (called Excellian) to 4 non-owned Allina organizations (3 clinics and 1 hospital), has received Meaningful Use payments for hospitals and eligible providers, and has been selected as a participant in the Pioneer ACO program. Allina would never have achieved these goals without technology governance structures and processes in place. Those technology structures started with relatively immature technology governance and have progressed to better organizational systems for decision making and guidance around IS initiatives. This case study will explore the journey from project governance to system governance and the lessons learned along the way.

APPROACH

In many ways, the deployment of the EHR across the system served as an opportunity to begin to bring all of the diverse operational entities together as a system. Many of the entities did not work together on a regular basis and the health system had only rudimentary structures or processes in place to facilitate collaborative decision making at the end-user level. The health system had just recently consolidated to a single board, which proved to be a significant positive factor in moving the EHR project forward.

EARLY GOVERNANCE

The project was established with a leadership and management structure that represented both clinical and business leadership and was operationally driven rather than IT driven, as portrayed in Figure 3-3. The chief medical officer was appointed to the senior executive sponsor role for the EHR implementation, reporting directly to the CEO for the project. The vice president role for the project was filled by a business operations leader who had led organization-wide change innovation projects, one of which was standardized revenue cycle work processes across the hospitals and the clinics. The rest of the management structure for the project consisted of eight directors, organized by function, to manage the work of the dedicated project team. The CIO and ad hoc IS leaders represented the IS department on the project PMO, ensuring alignment with IS strategy and direction.

Decision making for the design, development, and implementation of the EHR required a governance structure comprised of clinical and operation stakeholders working in conjunction with the dedicated EHR project team. Decision rights and a decision structure was developed as shown in Figure 3-4.

There was a desire to utilize existing committees/teams rather than duplicating structures. An inventory of existing organization-wide meetings/forums was taken. Those groups were factored into the governance structure for input and rec-

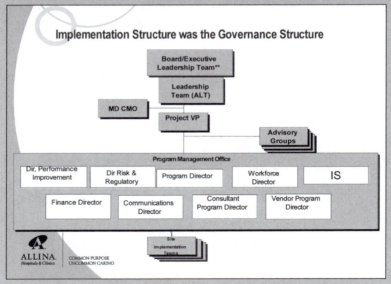

Reprinted with permission from Allina Hospitals & Clinics

Figure 3-3: Early Governance Structure

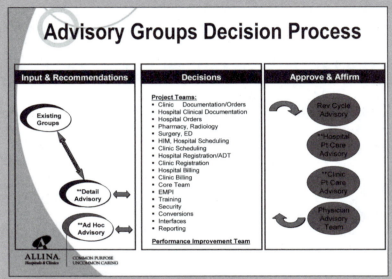

Reprinted with permission from Allina Hospitals & Clinics

Figure 3-4: Advisory Groups Decision Process

ommendations. In addition, each application formed a detailed advisory group (DAG) comprised of staff and leader subject matter experts from hospitals and clinics who would use the application (e.g., Pharmacy, ED). There was a goal to include representation from all 11 hospitals, and a wide cross-section of the 60-plus clinics in the DAGs. Based on time, travel, and resource availability, that goal was accomplished in varying degrees. The DAG's role was to:

- Provide subject matter expertise for the design of the application and related processes.
- Provide input to the project team throughout design, build, validation, implementation, and support phases of the project.
- Validate project team assumptions and recommendations related to workflow and the associated system build.
- Act as champions for the project.
- Support design and implementation of consistent processes across the system.
- Communicate design decisions with constituencies.

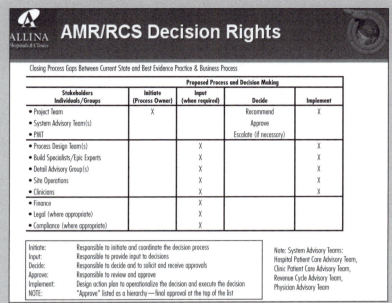

Figure 3-5: Decision Rights by Project Team

In some cases, an ad hoc DAG was formed to provide detailed input into a topic area that was a specialty within an application or that crossed applications.

Each application had a project team comprised of the full-time members of the overall EHR project team. Most of these staff members were end users from the business units who brought practical knowledge and expertise in the workflows and in meeting end-user needs. Because there wasn't standardization to all clinical and business workflows across all business units, the DAGs contributed a wider scope of input than the project team could provide. Decision rights for the design and build of the system was assigned to the project team for each application as shown in Figure 3-5.

Cross-departmental advisory groups were formed to provide operational oversight to the product and process design and implementation on a systemwide basis. Membership was comprised of organization leaders with subject matter expertise representative of operating departments across the system. The four advisory groups formed (called the "CATs") were Revenue Cycle Advisory Team (RCAT), Hospital Patient Care Advisory Team (HPCAT), Clinic Patient Care Advisory Team (CPCAT), and Physician Advisory Team (PAT). The CATs were chaired by organizational operation or executive leaders. Their responsibilities included the following:

- Provide directional leadership to guiding principles for design, process and product standardization, protocols/procedures, and prioritization of work effort.
- Act as champions for the project within their constituencies.
- Assist in addressing implementation and project resource barriers.
- Assist with issue resolution on a corporate/systemwide level.
- Provide input and recommendations regarding scope of objectives.
- Ensure project unification, goal achievement, and AMR/RCS (Automated Medical Record/Revenue Cycle System) integration.

The advisory groups were presented with integrated topic areas that crossed disciplines and departments and had final approval rights for the design. Their cross-discipline membership positioned the CATs to offer integrated perspective to the decisions made by each application's DAG and project team. They were used as an escalation forum when the project team needed organizational decisions that couldn't be made by the DAG or the project team. Criteria for decisions that were escalated to the advisory teams included:

- Exception to a guiding or design principle.
- Significant change to current state.
- Multidisciplinary change across departments/disciplines.
- Conflicting unresolved opinions between DAGs and project teams.

There was an additional component to the project structure that developed the clinical content of order sets to be used in hospitals. The Performance Improvement Team facilitated expert groups comprised of physicians, nurses, pharmacists, and other disciplines across the organization to develop and approve standardized order sets to be used for specific conditions and procedures. Guiding principles were developed to allow variation in order set content due to site-specific variables (e.g., variation in medications stocked at one hospital vs. another).

As the project moved from design and development to implementation, the advisory group structure (DAGs and CATs) played an evolving role. Strategies for implementation (big bang, sequence of rollout, etc.) were shared with the advisory groups to solicit stakeholder input from the hospitals and clinics. Training approaches were also presented for feedback. The DAGs provided forums for training content to be reviewed and validated, since the DAGs included end users who had developed knowledge of the system through the design and development phases of the project. Once implementation was underway, the advisory groups met with less frequency, being convened to share lessons learned from each implementation, provide input when a significant change to design was needed, and advise on requests to the EHR vendor for enhancements.

The Revenue Cycle System functions were being centralized in the organization in parallel to the EHR implementation. As a result, a centralized management structure was created. The new management team and committees provided the forums for EHR decisions to be made by the operations structure rather than continuing the interim project structures. Similar centralized management evolution did not occur with clinical operations.

Implementation of the EHR at each clinic and hospital required a local project governance structure to be developed, as shown in Figure 3-6. The types of decisions a site needed to make included training schedules, go-live plans, hardware placement, change management strategies, and workflow decisions. A typical site structure included a steering committee, project management team, and implementation team. Hospital implementations required a Patient Care Excellian Workgroup (PCEW), which included representation from all clinical areas. The PCEW made integrated workflow decisions for shared documentation and patient care processes and workflows that entailed handoffs between departments.

The original hardware plan for a site was created by a consultant, using industry standards. Following the experience at the

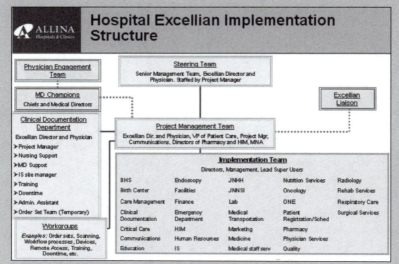

Reprinted with permission from Allina Hospitals & Clinics

Figure 3-6: Local Site Governance Structure

first hospital and first clinic, the plan was validated and rolled out to all sites (workstation in every exam room and in every hospital patient room). Decisions were made during a site walkthrough, with some flexibility accorded to the sites as long as the standards were maintained.

A site also needed to make decisions about some site-specific build configurations (e.g., default reports). The project management team packaged a listing of site decisions as part of the workflow sessions and worked with department representatives to arrive at local decisions.

MID-STAGE GOVERNANCE

By 2007, all of the metro hospitals and most of the clinics were live on the EHR, and a change in structure and governance was needed as the project and the organization moved into the support, stabilization, and optimization stages. The project advisory groups needed to transform into user groups shown in Figure 3-7, and an overhaul of the project structure was needed. As the project moved into the support mode, the number of staff was signifi-

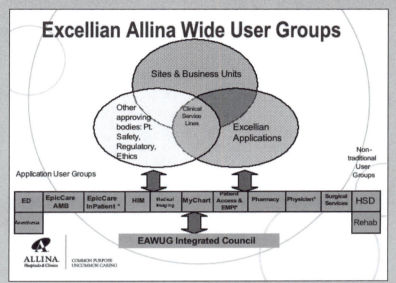

Reprinted with permission from Allina Hospitals & Clinics

Figure 3-7: Migration of User Groups

cantly reduced. The support model at the time included support staff at each hospital site that reported into the site's leadership. These staff remained at the site, but the reporting relationship was changed to a centralized structure, with a dotted line to site leadership. These site staff play a key role in keeping centralized and site groups aligned and in moving requests through the governance structure.

Some of the user groups' membership remained relatively intact as they moved from advisory groups to user groups. For example, the Physician User group membership and function stayed fairly stable, except for a new format in which one hour of the meetings changed to a combined agenda for decisions that affected ambulatory and inpatient, where both groups of physicians attended. Other groups required changes to membership to ensure that key areas were represented and the election of a formal leader who was not a member of the project team. At this time we also saw the addition of new groups, what we called "nontraditional user groups" such as Rehab and hospital service departments, that were aligned along a service line or a type of department rather than an application.

Although the role of the user groups continues to encompass design work, it is less of a major focus and more of a component of the work needed to prepare for yearly upgrades, incorporate new functionality, and contribute to optimization projects. The user groups provide a cross-organizational forum for shared problem solving and learning about functionality and workflows. Without formal operational decision rights, the user groups can only share practice suggestions. It is up to individual members to take best practice discussions back to their sites and advocate for implementation. When a best practice requires a system change that all sites must share, the user group forum is an effective decision-making structure that facilitates organization-wide consistent change. User groups are also instrumental in prioritizing the multiple requests for small system changes that are made, as well as large change requests that then go forward to the organizational governance groups for selection.

This period of time also saw the addition of the Integrated Council, an organizational level group with representatives from each of the user groups that is charged with making decisions on issues that affect multiple applications or making final decisions when two or more groups are not in agreement on how to move forward.

Shortly after the transition to the support and stabilization phase, the organization moved forward with a consolidation of the project team, IS, and health information management (HIM) into a single group. The need for structure and processes to support ongoing decision making around not only the EHR but IS and HIM initiatives was identified.

CURRENT STATE GOVERNANCE

Although the EHR remains a centerpiece of the IS initiatives at Allina, creating processes and structures that apply to all technology requests allows us to better serve our customers and create less confusion as to how and why decisions are made. At the same time, it creates excellent organizational and IS connections that provide input and review to the IS Strategic Plan, raises awareness of the potential overlap of IS and other organizational initiatives, and allows the organization to respond quickly to either stop, start, or re-prioritize work as needed—which has been invaluable during this year of changing federal initiatives.

Our current structure comprises the four main decision groups (leadership teams) shown in Figure 3-8, which represent clinical (CLT), business (BLT), privacy and security (HIPS) and infrastructure (ILT). IS adopted the idea for these groups from our existing clinical leadership team (CLT), a group of physicians (vice presidents of medical affairs) representing each business unit, chaired by the CMO. The role of these groups is to provide strategic direction to align business strategy with IS strategy; focus resources on system priorities in support of the achievement of strategies, goals, and performance targets; ensure IS investments increase business value and reduce business risk; and ensure good stewardship of resources.

We kicked off the process by spending one meeting discussing the problem statement and the group's roles and responsibilities. Although the governance groups were somewhat lukewarm to the idea at the beginning, thanks to the support of the CMO and other

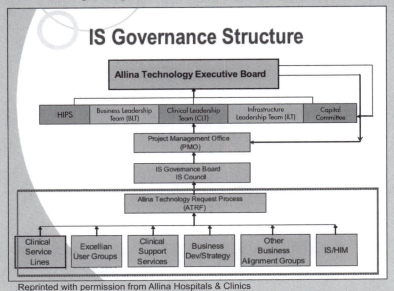

Reprinted with permission from Allina Hospitals & Clinics

Figure 3-8: Current Governance Structure

business leaders, they have embraced the methodology and have made a significant impact on making sure the right work is being done. A lesson learned from all of the groups is that it takes about three meetings for the group to gel and establish its rhythm. A significant amount of education and re-education is required to keep the groups moving, especially if there is turnover in membership.

Here's how it works: Once per quarter, IS has a standing item on each group's agenda for prioritization and decision making. Requests are initially vetted and prioritized through the user groups and the IS Governance Board and Council. Each request must have an executive sponsor who is responsible for educating his or her governance group member. The organization quickly realized that if it fails to educate its representative, the chance of the initiative moving forward is severely compromised. A prioritization grid is used to score requests for benefit to the organization and impact to resources. The grid includes sections to score for Patient Care Outcomes, Quality and Safety; Compliance, Contractual or Regulatory Requirements; Financial Benefit (cost savings, productivity improvement, cost of not implementing); Strategic Alignment and Measures of Caring; and Service Enhancement. IS prepares a list of all requests that includes a three-sentence summary along with benefit and impact scores. Additionally, a time line of all currently approved projects is provided, along with a number of available "slots." For example, four projects may be completing this quarter, which allows the Governance Group to select four new projects from all of the requests to add to the list. The initial limit for each group was randomly established based on knowledge of current levels of resource availability.

The feeder groups to the Leadership Groups continue to change and expand as the organization changes. Over the last few years, Allina has been developing Clinical Service Lines and, as they have matured, the technology governance structure has been able to accommodate their needs. All of these "requesting" groups fall under the label of Alignment Groups. Their purpose and rights and responsibilities are outlined in Figure 3-9. Some examples of these groups are the Diabetes Education Group, various steering committees such as Facilities, Human Resources, Lab, Pharmacy, Radiology, and Security, other approval groups such as the Clini-

Alignment Groups

Clinical Service Lines, Excellian User Groups, Clinical Support Services, Business Development and Strategy, Other Business Alignment Groups, IS and HIM

	Purpose	Decision Rights and Responsibilities
1	To identify business requirements and recommend IS application standards	• Recommend IS application standards, core applications, and technology solutions to IS Governance Board • Assist with ongoing adherence to standards within Allina
2	Prioritize project requests for area of responsibility. Request projects based upon business need and requirements.	• Prioritize projects • Recommend project work plan and requested timeline • Complete and submit technology requests (ATRF) for high priority projects.
3	Develop Business and strategic plans	• Develop business plans and communicate to IS Governance Board and/or IS Business Relationship Managers

ALLINA.
Hospitals & Clinics   COMMON PURPOSE
UNCOMMON CARING

Reprinted with permission from Allina Hospitals & Clinics

Figure 3-9: Alignment Groups

cal Nurse Practice Council, Business Transactions Committee, Regulatory/Compliance/Risk/Safety Committee, and the various service lines.

SUMMARY

In summary, technology governance and decision making continues to be an ongoing journey as the size and complexity of our technology implementations grow. We look to our governance structures to ensure that we are doing the right work and that we are making conscious and planned decisions about what work is deferred or prioritized. Additionally, the relationships that are forged with all of our customers have made the IS department a more informed and better partner in enabling the provision of the best care for our patients.

THE TRANSFORMATION PROCESS

Moving from the paper world to the electronic world is a process that needs to be nurtured and grown over time, watered like a flowering plant, ever so gently—watching carefully for new growth but aggressively cutting out dead leaves and rotting roots. Above all, it requires patience.

Sometimes you will encounter situations that will raise your hackles, but there are times when it's worthwhile to let things play out. At one organization, a member of the transformation team had been presenting an EHR update to CNOs and other nursing directors. She enthusiastically discussed the new clinical summary that provided real-time data at a glance, explaining to the directors how effective this tool would be for nursing hand-off.

This particular hospital had recently purchased equipment to record the nursing shift report and to have it available in a telephone system for retrieval. It was bewildering that the group did not wish to leverage real-time access to clinical data with a standardized template for easy hand-off. Luckily, the hospital was not planning to implement the telephone recording system for at least another six months, whereas implementation of the EHR was quickly approaching. The EHR Director knew from experience that the group wouldn't like the recorded shift report once they realized what access to real-time information would provide and what a great tool they would have at their disposal.

Nevertheless, the CNO called the EHR Director to reinforce the message that the nursing directors would not be implementing the EHR for hand-off but would be employing the recording tool instead. Rather than battle with him, the EHR Director decided to let them figure out on their own which system would be more advantageous. In the end, the implementation of the EHR went incredibly well. The system worked as designed, and the nursing staff loved the real-time clinical summaries.

Months later, the EHR Director was en route to the facility for a meeting when she recalled that now was about the time when they would begin using the recorded shift report. When she arrived at the meeting and asked about one of the nursing directors who was missing, she was told, "She's in a meeting to stop the implementation of the recording tool. We don't need it now that we have the EHR." That comment was an evolution. The flowering plant was blossoming; the rotting roots were gone.

FUNDING AND RESOURCE PLANNING

On a large project, taking into consideration size, scope, and impact on all levels of clinical operations, it's essential to have a clear funding and resource plan at the outset. Top leadership at impacted hospitals must be committed to providing the required financial resources for the entire duration of your project.

Having defined capital and operating money at the outset, securing it and making it available to the overall project plan for each year are key steps. When these steps are taken, no one has to go back and ask for additional money to fund the project. Nevertheless, you should prepare a financial forecast every quarter to ensure that you are managing your resources effectively. If it appears you might stray over the forecasted budget, you then have an opportunity to make real-time adjustments to get back on track.

At the initiation of one project, for example, there was no effective way to bring medical device information directly into the EHR. Two years into the project, the technology had matured and the healthcare system was ready to make an investment. Having the new technological capability proved to be a huge boost for productivity and efficiency.

Money-Saving Opportunities

When a method to proceed more effectively becomes apparent you should make adjustments to the overall plan, mid-stream if need be, before your budget review.

In some cases, such as when working with physicians, it is not clear at the outset what monetary resources will be required to help them succeed. To acclimate them to the new world of online documentation and order entry, for example, consider modeling a set of resource requirements that you refine as your project matures.

Over time, you may be able to take advantage of such opportunities as partnering with local colleges and universities, particularly hiring staff and interns and training them in the basics of EHR implementations. You might be able to identify other opportunities and ways of proceeding that you did not anticipate at the outset. This is normal in the course of a large project, but it's a likely occurrence on short-term, low-budget projects as well. It's critical to keep an eye out for opportunities to increase productivity, promote efficiency, and reduce costs wherever they arise, and be able to reallocate money as the need becomes apparent.

This constant process of recasting and reevaluating will help you to not only remain on budget, but actually to stay under budget in many cases. Staying under budget is useful when you present your project to stakeholders, customers, and other parties in the community. EHR implementations take considerable financial resources, and you will need to account for all expenditures in your fiduciary duty to members of the executive team and stakeholders.

Understandably, most readers don't have a multimillion-dollar budget to work with, but other funding options exist. As the implementation of EHRs was first mandated by then President George W. Bush in 2004[1] and reinforced by support from President Barack Obama in 2009 through passage of ARRA, the federal government has initiated several programs that provide funding support to organizations in need. Grant funds have been and are still available through federal and state agencies specifically to support the implementation of new health information technology, and there are incentive funds available through the CMS Meaningful Use Program. Regional Extension Centers (REC) provide support to physician practices throughout system selection, design, implementation, and training phases. All of these sources can and should be coordinated with affiliated health systems to ensure requirements are met to support health information exchange and other Meaningful Use requirements. In addition, most software vendors offer different price points based on a client's size and budget. There is a range of software available for large, mid-size, or small community hospitals. Based on the culture in your organization, its size, and its financial resources, you can mix and match your options.

Budget issues are obviously major. It takes money to drive transformation, and top executive leadership has to be willing to make the commitment.

PAYING FOR EXPERTISE

Freeing up professional staff away from their everyday duties to work on the project is an issue you will encounter. Many CEOs and chief financial officers (CFOs) say they would never shell out funds to take clinicians away from the patients' bedsides to work on a large-scale transformation inititative. But if you don't involve bedside clinicans in the design, you're not going to get engagement and adoption from frontline staff. This requires committing funds to backfill staff to work on the project.

If you ask frontline staff to make a choice, "Do I care for patients?" or "Do I work on this long-term project that will not occur in the immediate future?" they will always choose to care for patients. You should tell the executives in your organization that while it seems like a steep hurdle, if they're willing to make the commitment of pulling people away from their posts and involving them in the project in major ways, what they will achieve will more than offset the costs of moving around some of their staff.

Beyond simply bringing in talented clinical professionals, you should also recruit physicians to participate. You can't pay for every physician in the hospital to be involved, so seek physician champions who will serve as a liaison between the IT elements of the project and other physicians back in the hospitals. The role of physician champions is discussed in greater detail in Chapter 4.

PHYSICIAN ENGAGEMENT

Physician participation is vital to the success of any EHR implementation. A proven approach is to engage them early and often. Physician champions should receive compensation for the time they are pulled away from their posts.

The compensation rate should be comparable to their earnings in scheduling and treating patients. While their compensation can add up to a significant sum, it is important to budget for such funds because your success with physicians is critical to the project. Nothing is more powerful than having physicians talk to each other about the benefits of the transformation. Such discussions simply aren't the same coming from a nurse or other member of the healthcare delivery team.

Foster and nurture strong physician representation on all of your governance committees, ensuring that physicians have a strong stake in the game, are able to participate in decision making, and serve in an advisory capacity when necessary. Putting this in place will help achieve a successful clinical transformation.

A physician governance structure should include subcommittees comprised of representatives from all hospitals and/or departments within an individual hospital. They should meet on a regular basis to discuss key decisions and provide feedback about the usability of various aspects of the EHR. Any given hospital should have between four and ten physicians participating on the governing council or its subcommittees.

Recognize that the time of physicians, in the paid and unpaid categories, is valuable. Conduct meetings at times convenient to them. Compensated physicians may typically prefer meetings in the middle of the day. Uncompensated physicians usually prefer meetings in the evening. Hold such meetings in conference facilities within your respective hospitals. Treat physicians with consideration and respect, because they are key leaders and invaluable to the transformation process.

PLAYING IN THE SAME SANDBOX

Physicians and nurses dwell in the same world but sometimes find themselves at odds with one another. At this point in our society, physicians are still sometimes regarded as sacrosanct. For some, it's challenging to work collaboratively in a group with other members of the healthcare team who they might view as subservient, especially in community hospitals and rural settings. Other physicians have no problem with this. Resisters are sometimes seen by the project team as being in the "caboose of the train" as it relates to transformation. In time, they usually come around once they see the benefits and effects of their decisions in action.

For example, at one organization, nurses and nursing educators throughout the health system were part of a surgery department governance group that had been in place for several years prior to the EHR project. When the project started, the organization attempted to assemble a new multidisciplinary group that included both physicians and nurses from the surgery departments versus a separate nursing group. Friction occurred because both the physicians and the nurses claimed that they needed to go off and have discussions within their own groups and not come together to collaboratively make decisions. They did not see, prior to the EHR implementation, how their silo decisions would affect one another in the electronic world. So they remained in separate and distinct governance groups, with physicians in one group and nurses and ancillary clinicians in another group.

Three months or so after they went live with the system, both physicians and nurses changed their minds and said that they actually preferred being in one large collaborative governance group. A new combined group was finally initiated with physicians, nurses, and other members of the healthcare team all at the same table. Both physicians and nurses realized that they play in the same "sandbox" in the electronic world. If one party makes an update to the EHR, it impacts the other party. The physicians' EHR actions affected the nursing workflow, and what nurses did electronically could impact physicians' workflow.

After all is said and done, ownership is the key to successful adoption of the new processes and technologies. Each facility needs to take ownership of the measures and quality checks that ensure adoption of new processes prior to the go-live date as well as for years to come. Project managers and project management teams can provide support, but local ownership is essential to successful adoption and long-term cultural transformation.

INSIGHT AND LESSONS LEARNED

- The success of your major transformation initiative is dependent upon the degree to which those impacted by the organization's change serve in a governing capacity.
- In any large-scale implementation, an organization needs to have an effective model for decision making—or as it is referred to here, governance.
- Starting at the C-level, months in advance, visit each of your executives and win each over one by one. Keep them in the loop, especially as you approach a new phase.
- Because physician participation is vital, establish a structured approach to engage them early and often, and ensure strong physician representation on all governance committees.
- The project managers and project management teams can only do so much; ownership trumps all, and local ownership is key to successful adoption of the new processes and technologies.

THINKING FORWARD

1. Do you have your governance council established?
2. Is funding secured for your transformation project?
3. What are your decision framework and anchors for the transformation?
4. Who are your champions? Do you have physician champions?

5. Does your culture promote collaboration across the clinical disciplines?
6. Are your physicians engaged and compensated?

REFERENCE

1.   Ford EW, Menachemi N, Peterson LT, Huerta TR. Resistance is futile: but it is slowing the pace of EHR adoption nonetheless. *J Am Med Inform Assoc* 2009; 16(3):274-281.

CHAPTER 4

Achieving Buy-in at Every Level

INTRODUCTION

In this pivotal chapter, we cover the approach to take to induce all of the role players who want to be a part of this transformation and how to involve employees from the outset. The key to transformation is a constant focus on leadership, effective governance, and frontline engagement. All of your activities and strategies should be fully integrated with your health system's model for evaluating performance, from the executive level through the employee level.

Since using an EHR to transform an organization is a high-quality initiative, every aspect should be tied into your health system's vision. The objectives, scope of work, methodology, and framework should follow a transformation model such as the one illustrated in Chapter 2 or a similar model to help guide your organization's transition to the future state.

The implementation of an EHR is an opportune time to examine and update workflows to take advantage of the capabilities of new systems. As such, leaders must encourage a culture of continual ongoing improvement, and end users must be engaged to provide their input. You should select a name for the transformation project itself that has significant meaning to your organization and its culture. As a positive first step in achieving buy-in, you might even consider holding a vote, with employees selecting the name.

GET EVERYONE INVOLVED

To make the project a success, ensure that all employees have a role to play and that they know their responsibilities. It's important to identify these roles up front so that everyone is aware of what's expected of them going into the project. Sharing the details of an implementation with all stakeholders is a key success factor. In providing clear direction for the various role players, each group must be identified and targeted for definitive communication.

As you develop your transformation program, focus on the roles and responsibilities of everyone who will be impacted: the project team, executive leadership, hospital employees, and customers. This includes anyone who will work with the EHR, from senior leaders and clinicians to physicians (e.g., hospitalists, residents, affiliated and unaffiliated) starting from the first day that they are in your organization. Map out strategies for socializing strategic messages with key executives, important customers, and members of the project team. Make sure that all team members are aware of their responsibilities in the transformation program initiative.

No group should be left out. The participation level of these groups dictates how well, as a project leader, you'll be able to achieve your own goals on the project. The titles that you ascribe to the various players can be formal, but should help in discerning who's who. Moreover, the role players in a major transformation initiative can be stratified many different ways. For example:

Stakeholder: Anyone with a vested interest in seeing the project succeed, including the initial authorizing party, which could be the CEO. Stakeholders also can include top managers, other department and division heads within the organization, vendors, patients, clinicians, physicians, and the community at large.

Authorizing Party: The person or persons who initiate a project. These are sometimes called sponsors, but this can be inaccurate terminology since sponsors might have little to do with the project after initiation.

Project Manager: This is the person (or persons) who, following the lead from the authorizing party to initiate the project, produces the scope of work and timelines for accomplishing the overall project objective. The project manager also plots the intended use of resources, including labor, equipment, and allocated funds.

Project Team Member: Within any project management team, this is a staff member who performs assigned work. Within a larger organization, a team member could represent an employee who is not directly connected with the project management team but still has a role to play in the project.

Targets of Transformation: People who will be impacted by the project and the impending changes.

Physician Champions: Physicians who have taken an active role in learning and employing the system, have the capability to serve as role models to others, can answer questions, and can explain elements of the system to physicians.

Super Users: This group includes anyone who is knowledgeable, enthusiastic, and supportive of the new system; can deftly explain elements of it to others; and serves as a continual, on-site advocate. Depending on the department, the ratio of super users to other employees varies widely. Super users complete special training and provide "at-the-elbow" support during and after activations. These system experts are advocates for improvements in usability. A good model is one or two super users per department.

Subject Matter Experts (SME): This group engages at the operational level. SMEs drill down to the details and work to ensure that each step in the redesign of every department's workflow is accounted for, leaving nothing to chance. As SMEs grow in their knowledge of the new system, in many cases they transition to the role of super user. Their role is crucial to the success of any EHR implementation.

THE ORGANIZATIONAL TRANSFORMATION TEAM

Establishing an Organizational Transformation Team (OTT) is a critical step that should be accomplished early on to help promote a culture of change as well as urgency. This team is the foundation for transformation management initiatives and focuses on managing organizational adoption and evaluating readiness, training, physician adoption, and communications. The essence of clinical transformation—aligning people, processes, and technology to advance clinical care with the goal of improving care delivery and the quality of that care—is the core work and oversight of this team.

The OTT oversees all of the organizational change management activities during the transformation process. It comprises:

- Members from the clinical transformation team, including a physician adoption expert.
- Communications experts.
- Training managers.
- EHR directors.
- Experts in change management.

Many of these positions will be filled internally; however, if your organization lacks the appropriate expertise, you will have to hire external staff. Note that roles can also be combined for smaller organizations.

The OTT provides oversight for all of the activities described in this chapter. It leads the organization's efforts by providing expertise and assistance in a variety of ways:

- Promotes the need for change management and introduces the concept of planned and intentional change.
- Establishes baseline goals that help set the tone for the implementation and gauge its success. Thereafter, measurements against these goals should be taken at various times throughout the program's life cycle to determine how well the activities are actually working.
- Develops, implements, and monitors the workflow review process.
- Oversees communication planning and monitoring of communication effectiveness.
- Provides focus on the training approach of the organization (including the need to own the transformation and workflow changes) and the measurement of training effectiveness.

EFFECTIVE COMMUNICATION

Communication at critical junctures with all teams on all levels is fundamental to the success of the project. As previously discussed, retaining a marketing or advertising firm well-versed in healthcare organization communications helps develop key messages to be disseminated to employees, physicians, facility leadership, and patients. Messages should include the "what's in it for me" type of benefit. Take a close look to make sure your message is in user-friendly terms, not in IT terms.

You should constantly strive, in the plainest English possible, to convey the benefits that the recipients of the message will receive as the result of the major changes coming, how the patients will benefit, and how the entire health system itself will benefit.

It's important to recognize that different hospitals have different leadership styles and different cultures. Take these approaches into account to keep your communication strategies on target. Use multiple presentations in a variety of meetings, distribute newsletters, publish time lines, and celebrate successes and milestones. All of these initiatives are important to helping your organization continue to move forward along the adoption curve.

Early in the project, communication from the CEO helps sets the tone for the importance of the project and its vision. Absolute transparency and honesty are critical to maintaining credibility. You have to anticipate the instructions and support that each group needs and the timing of the messages that you'll offer.

Assessing Readiness: Survey for Feedback
Some groups within some organizations are more responsive or more ready to proceed than others. Without knowing the group's state of readiness, you're "fishing in the dark." A transformation program survey, distributed systemwide to all employees, helps gauge the level of organizational readiness based on focus areas, department, and even facility.

In addition, use benchmarks and measures related to readiness by surveying clinicians, physicians, and facility leadership to gauge how ready they are for the impending transformation. Query respondents to a degree that will allow you to find the pockets of resistance; then you will know where to devote extra time. In some cases you may even know the likely level of resistance person by person, although nobody should be required to identify themselves.

Below are some guidelines to use when creating surveys:
- Glean key questions, then administer mini-versions of the surveys, refine them and only then employ them institution-wide. With any survey, make sure that it's tied into other initiatives going on in the organization.
- Make sure the surveys are easy to complete. Use the answers "strongly disagree, disagree, neutral, agree, strongly agree," so that people can quickly enter check marks in boxes online.
- When you complete a survey, share the results to provide a current snapshot of affairs. This allows you to illustrate to each department how staff is progressing in terms of overall adoption, as well as provide before-and-after indicators.

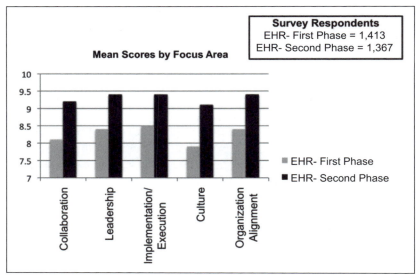

Figure 4-1: Transformation Management Readiness Survey Results by Focus Area

• Once you've administered the survey, analyze the data to provide focused intervention where necessary.

The example from one organization presented in Figure 4-1 indicates the results of 332 survey respondents across five criteria, including collaboration, leadership, implementation/execution, culture, and organization alignment. Participants indicated how ready they believed their department to be during pre-implementation. A follow-up survey mid-implementation with 232 respondents tabulated two years later indicates a higher degree of readiness for the five focus areas in question.

GEAR MESSAGES ACCORDINGLY

With each group impacted, identify the critical success factors, down to the individual task level. Determine the appropriate goals, the risks associated with striving for such goals, and how to diminish potential risks. Inform employees of process changes that will impact them, including start and stop issues—tasks that they need to stop doing, tasks that they need to start doing, and tasks that represent ongoing, future-state activities. Such start-and-stop issues can have an effect on their daily workflow activities, as depicted in Table 4-1.

Process	Stop	Start	Continue
Nursing Admission Assessment	Nurse: Documenting patient education on paper	Nurse: Assessing and documenting education needs on Patient Education form in EHR	
	Clinician: Documenting multi-disciplinary discharge planning on paper	Nurse: Assessing and documenting discharge needs on Admission Assessment form in EHR	
	Nurse: Documenting initial pain assessment on paper	Nurse: Assessing and documenting pain assessment and vital signs in EHR flowsheet	Nurse: Documenting Admission assessment and head to toe assessment on admission
Evidence Based Nursing (EBN) - Pressure Ulcer Prevention	Nurse: Documenting and calculating Braden Score on paper	Nurse: Assessing and documenting risk for pressure ulcer using Braden Score on the Admission assessment in the EHR Score is automatically calculated upon signing the form electronically	Nurse: Documenting Braden Score daily

Table 4-1: Stop, Start, Continue Process Analysis

Although this requires considerable effort—constantly interacting with each group, recruiting talented insiders, and having them help you map out a plan—it enables you to create a path for virtually everyone, in all departments, at all times. The right communication at the right time, vertically, from the top down, and horizontally, from peer to peer, reinforces what needs to be done.

Be diligent in crafting messages geared for different groups. For physicians, for example, focus on the kinds of questions and concerns that they would logically have such as, "What is the patient going to receive from this?" or "Why is this project important to me?" The answer should be: "You gain timely access to information and the ability to diagnose more quickly and effectively."

Ready Responses

Rather than requiring months of work effort, the process of crafting such key messages can take only a few weeks. Train your project team members on how to convey key messages so when team members are out and about, in groups or one-on-one, they know how to respond. For example, if a project team member is visiting a physician's office and the physician says, "Why should I do this? What is this going to mean for me?" on the spot, your team member can offer highly effective answers.

To prepare team members, engage them in role-playing activities. One person poses as a tough physician asking one difficult question after another, while a second team member remains calm and answers each concern. When you practice this model, you see that when team members are confronted in the real world, they do not need notes to help with answers—they know the messages cold and provide appropriate responses to the tough questions. What's more, when you make rounds at hospitals during go-lives and talk to employees about the new system, they are able to describe their experiences using the key messages. This is an indication that you have clearly and effectively communicated the messages.

PHYSICIAN ADOPTION STRATEGIES

Because physicians play a vital role in the success of the transformation initiative, allocate considerable attention to them. In terms of their daily routine, focus on that which typically matters most to physicians: the ability to have rapid, user-friendly access to the information they need, when and where they need it.

Strong physician leadership and support of physician governance is essential to achieve buy-in from the broad swath of physicians engaged in any health system. Such support can lead to medical staff that is committed to and engaged in both the methodology and technology associated with the new system. All the while stay focused on what's in it for physicians and diligently answer their questions, such as "How does the new system support my workflow and help me to improve efficiency?"

Physician Champions

Physician champions are physicians who take an active role in learning and using the system and have the capability to serve as role models for others.

When you invest in recruiting physicians off the line for a few hours—when they'd otherwise be taking care of patients—you end up developing true advocates. During your time together, teach them the basics of the software and discuss the fundamentals of organizational transformation management. As always, show them what's in it for them, and paint an accurate picture of what they can expect in the future.

Later, when your physician champions are in conversations with other physicians, the words they use regarding this change will go a long way in increasing acceptance. Some of the buy-in you will achieve with hospital physicians won't occur without your physician champions favorably influencing them. Because the champions have the physician perspective, they are able to make valuable contributions to the design team. When elements of the system work for them, you know they will work for others.

Ideal Characteristics of Physician Champions:
1. Clinically respected physicians and clinicians.
2. Preferably have a track record of being successful transformation agents.
3. Team players with other clinical disciplines.
4. Organizational strategic thinkers, rather than ones focused on their own department or specialty.
5. Clinicians who like to teach and have strong, personable communication styles that can adapt to differing audiences.
6. Available, interested, and enthusiastic.
7. Experience in a leadership position (e.g., department chair or directorate lead).

Does all this time, energy, and money spent with the physicians and frontline staff (not to mention pulling these individuals away from their primary roles to be involved in the change initiative) result in increased efficiency? The answer is yes. One of the keys to success is developing a robust set of performance metrics starting in the first phase of the EHR implementation and using them to describe progress and pain points along the way. This is one of the most effective data-driven ways to communicate the direct impact of the physicians and frontline staff to those who are internal to the process and to external stakeholders. Performance metrics are discussed in greater detail in Chapter 8.

Find Out What They Have to Say

Take a careful look at physicians and what they have to say. As mentioned earlier, survey them in a variety of venues to assess their transformation readiness. In these surveys ask about their level of satisfaction with the usability of the EHR. Also look at how they are using

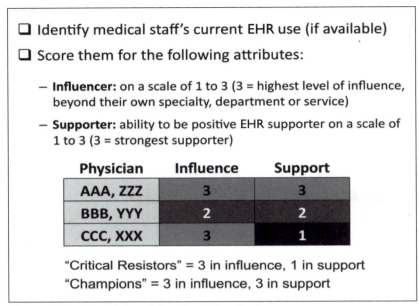

❑ Identify medical staff's current EHR use (if available)

❑ Score them for the following attributes:

— **Influencer:** on a scale of 1 to 3 (3 = highest level of influence, beyond their own specialty, department or service)

— **Supporter:** ability to be positive EHR supporter on a scale of 1 to 3 (3 = strongest supporter)

Physician	Influence	Support
AAA, ZZZ	3	3
BBB, YYY	2	2
CCC, XXX	3	1

"Critical Resistors" = 3 in influence, 1 in support
"Champions" = 3 in influence, 3 in support

Figure 4-2: Physician Adoption Monitoring

the system, such as the number of clicks they use to enter orders, and work closely with those who are struggling with the new tools.

With physicians—and this holds true for other role players and teams—use a variety of tools and processes to assess where they are and how far they have to go on the transformation curve. Develop a physician stakeholder matrix as depicted in Figure 4-2. This tool focuses on such critical criteria as level of influence, high-volume admitting physicians, and how comfortable and supportive they are with using the EHR, and then ranks them. This will allow you to focus on this group of physicians since their use of the EHR will have the greatest impact on your organization. Use the matrix to develop an action plan around each of these physicians to monitor their progress, particularly if you identify physicians who may need more assistance and encouragement than others. This tool will also help you identify potential physician supporters who can help champion the change and influence physicians who may not be as supportive and excited about the impending changes.

Should you do this analysis with everyone within your healthcare system? No, this is not practical. Because physicians carry much weight and have significant influence on operations and revenue, you should be more particular in terms of assessing their readiness and developing an action plan for assisting them with adoption.

With physicians, who essentially give you business, options abound for keeping tabs. You can consult the medical staff services within a facility. These staff members have the responsibility of hiring and credentialing physicians and, therefore, know them well. It's easy for them to tell you in advance who is enthusiastic about the system and who is decidedly not, who is going to be resistant, and who might need some extra attention. They may also point out to you lead physicians who can help champion others along. You should also leverage your physician champions to help gauge physician readiness and to develop a plan for dealing with resistors. Even if your organization is small, you can leverage the resources you have to accomplish this.

Make Training Mandatory

Making physician training part of the fabric of the organization will help to establish a new norm while weeding out those few who do not cooperate. It's essential to have such conversations up front and to secure buy-in from this group early on. Otherwise, you run the risk of encountering confusion, dissension, and unnecessary resistance later, and spending more time and effort than if you had simply established this ground rule at the outset. Physicians who are leaders can be extremely useful in making sure others are on board.

At one organization, our goal was to make physician training mandatory; either they take the EHR training or they don't practice. To be frank, we were skeptical that such a mandate would fly. When we presented the plan to a group of senior leaders, the Vice President of Medical Affairs chimed in with his support. The other heavy hitters in the group immediately echoed his sentiments, suggesting that we work together to establish a common procedure for approaching the medical committees that would emphasize the training requirement for physicians.

CASE STUDY:
LEVERAGING PHYSICIAN ENGAGEMENT
FOR CPOE IMPLEMENTATION

By Alastair MacGregor, MB ChB, Chief Information Officer,
Chief Medical Informatics Officer, and Chief Information Officer
Methodist Le Bonheur Healthcare

INTRODUCTION

Methodist Le Bonheur Healthcare (Le Bonheur) in Memphis, Tennessee, commenced a journey in 2008 to achieve physician adoption of computerized provider order entry (CPOE) in a phased implementation of an EHR across its hospitals. While we encountered a number of challenges, high levels of medical staff adoption of CPOE and positive measureable benefits emerged in 2011.

BACKGROUND

Methodist Le Bonheur Health System is a blend of academic and community-based facilities in an integrated delivery network consisting of seven hospitals (including a major academic medical center for the University of Tennessee Health Science Center), a network of ambulatory facilities and services, and more than 2,000 affiliated physicians. In addition, the organization has a second academic partnership with the University of Memphis that led to establishment of centers for healthcare technology, leadership, and healthcare economics during the past decade. The health system has more than 1,600 hospital beds and specialty areas that include a brain and spine institute, transplant institute, cancer center, and the Le Bonheur Children's Hospital, all serving the Mid-South region.

Physician leadership for every health system is critical. The key health system level physician leaders for Methodist Le Bonheur included the operational CMOs at each of the hospitals. In collaboration with these leaders, I focused on CPOE design, rollout planning, championing, and ensuring physician adoption of the EHR and CPOE over the last three years.

GOVERNANCE

We applied a multidisciplinary approach to the governance activities and process for the full system implementation. Governance groups at each hospital, along with executive corporate leadership, were responsible for: aligning organizational imperatives, developing performance measures and goals, serving as executive physician and nursing sponsors, and establishing accountability for deliverables and time lines throughout the project. The Medical Executive Committee (MEC), along with the Multidisciplinary Orders Clearinghouse, made all final decisions on policies and process changes to achieve the most positive impact on patient safety, outcomes, and operational performance. I recognized the need to strengthen cultural discipline early on and set forth a number of mantras during system design sessions, one of which was, "You can have anything you want, but you will all agree you want it."

PROJECT IMPLEMENTATION

In 2008 Le Bonheur's leadership was engaged in the implementation of a Cerner Millennium EHR. For the health system, planning for CPOE implementation was a very high priority. A number of activities were essential for securing physician engagement that included:

- Establishing physician-specific governance that included CMOs, multispecialty and multidisciplinary clinical service groups, and additional medical staff champions appointed on a fee-for-service basis.
- Developing specific targeted physician change management initiatives and communications.
- Making CPOE an enterprise-wide clinical and medical requirement.
- Requiring medical staff training and competency that was tracked and fed back to medical and administrative leaders. Changes were approved by the MEC to add the requirement for EHR/CPOE training and use of CPOE to Medical Staff By-Laws.
- Requiring electronic signature by physicians except during downtime.

- Driving physician participation in design and workflow decisions.
- Defining pre- and post-implementation physician adoption metrics.
- Developing detailed planning for continuing physician education and adoption.

Another activity that was important for CPOE implementation was physician and clinical staff engagement planning for order set development and maintenance. We planned for 60 hours of development time (e.g., identifying potential components, drafting order sets, gaining consensus, publishing, and gaining feedback) for each order set and an additional 35 hours for order set maintenance.

Throughout the project, there were several keys to success. The first was the selection of physician champions, along with the identification of physician influencers, supporters, and resistors at each hospital, which I led along with each hospital's CMO. Critical characteristics of these champions included being recognized as change agents, strategic thinkers, strong communicators, and having the availability and enthusiasm for the EHR/CPOE initiative. Putting *systemness* at the heart of the implementation approach, empowering the physician community, keeping patient safety at the forefront of all key decisions, and providing recognition for time and efforts in leading change on the EHR and CPOE implementations were additional keys to success.

Physician and clinician training education and appreciation of workflow changes are critical elements of every EHR/CPOE implementation. At Methodist Le Bonheur, the requirement for completing physician EHR/CPOE training and maintaining competency levels was incorporated into physician credentialing and Medical Staff By-Laws across the health system. Additionally, a requirement was put in place for all physicians to be re-credentialed every two years.

The MEC and local medical leadership empowered the corporate EHR/CPOE training teams to ensure that training methodologies included: assessment of physician training needs; 100 percent online session for physicians, with a blend of online, classroom, and office-based training for larger groups; a target of 90 percent core medical staff to be trained for go-live and one-on-one support at go-live and for supplemental training; and tools for daily tracking and feedback status reports on completion of training and ongoing competency testing.

As a result in 2009, 1,523 medical staff were trained, with one percent receiving their training online. In 2010, 2,172 medical staff were trained, with 93 percent having completed training online. By 2011, 100 percent of the medical staff were trained online, as were pharmacy staff. A number of factors supported this increased use of online training:

- 24/7 convenient access.
- Ease of use for refresher training.
- Approved CME credits for completing training and competency.
- Easier maintenance of content.
- Reduced requirement for access to training rooms.
- Added value for office staff and inpatient nursing.
- Reduced full-time equivalents (FTEs) for educators to meet physician training requirements.

LESSONS LEARNED

We established governance and ground rules to mitigate risks of failure and unintended consequences; however, we encountered several challenges throughout our EHR implementations. Barriers existed in several areas, including: variation in leadership commitment, facility architectures, and early support for innovation; past negative experiences with information system implementations; knowledge transfer of best practices; disenfranchisement with corporate headquarters; and the lack of standardized paper order sets. To deal with these challenges, we undertook several actions that included local staff empowerment, well-defined objectives and time lines, and consistent communications with the physician community and staff.

As a result of these challenges and actions, there were a number of lessons learned from the project in 2011. In the training domain, online training and the process for getting EHR/CPOE training approved to count as continuing medical education (CME) proved to be huge wins with the physician community.

Publishing names of trained and untrained staff proved to be a reinforcement tactic for driving participation in required training. Other lessons learned included the following:

- Balance project plans against clinical needs—important.
- Do not assume that every hospital will be diligent in readiness preparation.
- Train hospital analysts in customer service especially related to diagnosis of issues and management of the issue.
- Establish clear plans and policies for downtime.
- Ensure that a hospital system health maintenance plan (e.g., reports and tasks) is in place for the post-conversion period.
- Establish an equitable and transparent issue management process.

METRICS

The leadership team recognized the importance of establishing pre- and post-conversion metrics to evaluate physician adoption of the EHR and CPOE. In planning to establish meaningful metrics for the system, the team established:

- Operational owners for data collection.
- Design of data collection tools.
- Design of automated reports to track post go-live trends.

Key elements that Methodist Le Bonheur focused on for qualitative and quantitative metrics that produced insights included:

- Utilization rates of CPOE and other new applications.
- Process efficiencies such as turnaround times and staff efficiencies.
- Clinical outcomes.
- User satisfaction.

As the MEC ensured that local leadership was made accountable for key metrics, a goal of 80 percent was set for inpatient CPOE post-conversion physician adoption and 90 percent for ED CPOE adoption. In 2011, with all facilities having CPOE implemented, CPOE adoption was reported at above 90 percent for all ED settings. Several other metrics were tracked for the pre- and post-implementation stages. In many cases, we gathered baseline data a year in advance of the implementation to help understand the progress being made later on. Table 4-2 provides a subset of many metrics that were evaluated.

These metrics are only a small segment of the full suite of metrics that we evaluated. These original measurements helped give the MEC and each facility's clinical leadership insights on progress being made with physician adoption, as well as quality and safety initiatives at each facility related to the EHR/CPOE implementation. Other key areas that we evaluated included medication administration and adverse drug events, which provided even deeper insights for clinical leadership to understand both the levels of adoption and specific processes and systems that needed to be continually refined for the benefit of physicians and their patients.

The lessons learned and benefits realized provide evidence of progress and adoption by the Mid-South physician community. The Methodist Le Bonheur EHR/CPOE implementation has been highly successful, and physician adoption across all seven hospitals has demonstrated improved patient safety and the quality of care for the health system's patients and the community of Memphis, Tennessee.

Measure Description	Evaluation Period	Goal/ Baseline*	Measurement
Inpatient CPOE Adoption Rate	Feb-May 2010	N/A	88.1%
Emergency Department CPOE Adoption Rate	Feb-May 2010	Goal: 90.0%	89.5%
Percentage of Medical Dose Alerts versus Orders	Feb-May 2010	Baseline: 14.4%	18.6%
Admission Assessment Captures: Allergy Information	Feb-May 2010	Baseline: 67.4%	82.2%
Admission Assessment Captures: Height	Feb-May 2010	Baseline: 74.3%	85.7%
Formulary Compliance: CPOE Problem Entries	Feb-May 2010	Baseline: 0.07%	0.03%
Medical Staff Satisfaction: "Allows me to be more effective and efficient to provide safe care." Answer category: *slightly agree*	Feb-May 2010	Baseline: 32.0%	35.0%

* Baselines stated are for the time period January–November 2009.

Table 4-2: Methodist Le Bonheur Pre- and Post-Implementation CPOE Metrics

THE IMPORTANCE OF SUPER USERS

Super users are clinical end users who have had extra training and who have proven themselves to be effective in the ability to communicate.

Super users have a positive attitude. They like explaining things and helping to train people. They have a good understanding of the clinical workflow. What's more, they understand the importance of the EHR and are ready to serve as its advocates.

Super users might have been part of the actual design team and may have started in a subject matter expert role. Regardless of where they're drawn from, they play a vital role in ensuring an EHR's success. A general rule of thumb is that they should represent approximately 10 percent of your workforce.

Super users represent the "eyes and ears" in the field. They operate at times and places where the implementation team simply can't be present, because no team could stretch itself that thin. Because super users are able to blend their knowledge of clinical operations, workflow, and system functionality, they provide a level of support to end users that enables them to troubleshoot complex issues.

Super users tend to have a unique ability for rapid problem identification, as well as resolution. They know how to nip problems in the bud before they have a chance to escalate. Regard them as pivotal to systemwide adoption as well as optimization. Organizations that struggle with adoption and waver from the original standard workflow design will most likely have super users that are no longer engaged. That's because super users are critical for ongoing optimization activities and hardwiring the transformation. Chapter 5 focuses on both recruiting and working with super users.

METHODOLOGY AND TOOLS

Efficiency gained by redesigning workflow and processes can create an active, engaged culture among staff and provide benefits for years to come. Once you begin this journey, it never ends. As hospitals and physician offices ramp up an EHR, they should map out their current state processes to enhance the design of their future state processes. Over time, organizations can continue to review their processes to make improvements.

Through the design process, you should document the current workflow throughout all clinical and administrative departments that use or interface with any element of the EHR, and then determine which steps can be eliminated as a result of using new applications in the design of future state workflows. After the system is implemented, the future state design documents can be used to validate the results.

Process and workflow redesign are only successful, however, when they are aligned with organizational transformation management efforts. Following are some tools for ensuring that this takes place and achieving buy-in along the way.

Moving Workflows into Practice

In Chapter 3, we discussed how subject matter experts at the governance levels help develop and win approval for future state of workflow. You should take those approved future state workflows to a facility six months before go-live. Walk the players through the workflows, carefully explaining the forthcoming transformation. You should explain what the changes will mean for those individuals, as well as how others are going to be impacted.

Spell out which activities will stop, which will continue, and which will start. To do a thorough job, spend a few weeks at each facility if possible and, depending on the amount of change, focus attention on the local culture. Although this can be time consuming, the benefits are worthwhile. You will most likely stumble upon bad processes that need to be fixed in advance of implementations. Use your super users to co-lead these sessions; you will find they are pivotal for adoption and buy-in. When employees see their super users walking them through the new workflows, they gain confidence.

As a result of rolling out one hospital after another, you will need to incorporate lessons learned and insights as you move forward. Engage a facility's senior leadership at the C-suite level, early and often, to obtain buy-in and help set the tone within facilities before you arrive for activation.

Once the frontline teams design the future state workflows and the governance groups approve them, proceed *department by department* to identify any wrinkles that could hamper implementation progress well before it begins. Most go-live issues tend to be process-related rather than technology-related.

For example, sometimes hospitals have no common approach to documenting such items as medication administration. One organization we encountered had created a flow sheet to document weekly medication administration, but they were unable to achieve agreement on a standardized preprinted 24-hour medication administration record (MAR).

We weren't able to design a MAR specifically for them on the fly, but we did prepare a helpful, high-level work process that would meet their needs and the needs of other facilities for a common approach. They were able to go from using a seven-page paper medication record to a streamlined, 24-hour standardized, preprinted paper MAR.

About two weeks into the implementation, and feeling as if the transition would be too much, they reported problems with the new standardized preprinted MAR. They said it was taking too long for their nurses to document and, therefore, their productivity was being unnecessarily hindered. When we examined the situation, we saw that they had built a series of conditional orders, resulting in an 18-page printed MAR. From this experience, we realized that we needed to understand, on a hospital-by-hospital basis, the detailed procedures of departments, floor by floor. This is a critical success factor in the transformation process.

Your mission is to work with end users to help make appropriate system refinements so they become increasingly confident when meeting with a new group in the next facility or department. Once the software is proven and the system is working in one place, you have a ready demonstration model and a key tool to encourage buy-in at the next facility.

Standardization at the Local Level

Assemble teams of clinicians and methodically examine each of their future state processes. Using the medication process as an example, explain what it will be like in the future and how the new system could make clinicians' lives easier. Prepare hands-on demonstrations so that they can see, feel, and touch the system elements before implementation. Then watch the light bulbs go on. Users will ask, "What about this?" and "What about that?" Often, they identify relevant issues that you weren't aware of but need to address. Document issues that arise during the demonstrations and present them to facility leadership teams who can then develop solutions in advance. This helps ensure that implementations will be as smooth as possible.

Build the model and then ensure that it works at every facility. Much like how McDonald's® sends staff to "Hamburger University" and strives to offer the same experience over and over to every customer who walks in the door, standardize your processes. This guarantees that those doing the same job have access to the same body of information and receive the same type of guidance.

CASE STUDY:
A CULTURE OF COLLABORATION
TO ACHIEVE PROCESS IMPROVEMENT

By Jane E. Renwick, MSA, BSN, RN-BC, NEA-BC,
Director, Enterprise Applications, Trinity Health

INTRODUCTION

Trinity Health is one of the largest Catholic health systems in the United States. Inspired by our Catholic faith tradition and a vision to be distinguished by an unrelenting focus on clinical and service outcomes, we seek to create excellence in the care experience. This is realized through a commitment to our patients to share their journey to health and to be their most trusted health partner for life. As a faith-based health system, we are devoted to a ministry of healing, serving persons through a network of hospitals, healthcare services, and partnerships at the community, regional, and national levels—with a focus on improving healthcare delivery. The system includes 20 Ministry Organizations (MOs) encompassing 49 hospitals (37 owned, 12 managed) in 10 states with more than 56,000 full-time equivalent employees, more than 11,000 active staff physicians, and more than 10,000 nurses. Trinity has revenues of $9 billion and provided more than $453 million in community benefit in 2011.

In 2000, Trinity began a journey to unite state-of-the-art computer information systems with best-practice processes across the health system in three areas: clinical, revenue, and resource planning (supply chain). "Genesis" is Trinity Health's solution to create the healthcare system of the 21st century. Goals of the clinical component of Genesis include increasing patient safety and quality of care through utilization of evidence-based, decision-making tools and standardized best practices processes. The journey transformed patient care delivery through the integration of best practice clinical practice with leading edge technology. Genesis is a major strategic capital investment in excess of $400 million over 10 years. A focus on best practice involves the redesign of 300-plus business and clinical processes with the implementation of more than 30 applications (clinical, revenue, supply chain). Genesis changes the workflow for over 80 percent of the hospital employees and 100 percent of physicians. Trinity's big-bang implementation model has enabled us to emerge as a leading adopter of health IT among community hospital systems. An implementation of this scale requires careful planning, execution, and evaluation.

Trinity has established a comprehensive Readiness Change Management process. It is a structured, repeatable process that is critical to ensuring that personnel, processes, and local infrastructure is prepared for the implementation of Genesis. This methodology has enabled Trinity to achieve a very aggressive implementation time line. Readiness is focused on operational aspects of the project (people, process, technology, and culture) to drive organizational change—not system implementation alone. The methodology is specifically designed to minimize the risk of adversely impacting operations when the new systems are implemented and to maximize the ability of each ministry organization to achieve the operational benefits of best practices and new systems. A key component contributing to Trinity's successful transformation is its relentless focus on process excellence.

GENESIS PROCESS INTEGRATION STRATEGIES

Efficient, effective clinical processes in acute care hospitals are crucial to achieving the goal of excellence in care experience. The implementation of an EHR should not focus on technology alone, as this is insufficient to achieve long-lasting clinical transformation. Trinity Health has incorporated an entire layer of process improvement into its readiness methodology. The addition of the following process strategies has been a key enabling component in the success of Genesis throughout our health system.

- Executive process continuum orientation.
- Role delineation.
- Product overview/early application training.
- Process excellence training.
- Integrated process review.

- Process drill down/finalization.
- Process simulation.
- Integration of process into training.
- Go-live process support.
- Post-activation review.

Executive Process Continuum Orientation

The integration of process begins early in Trinity's Genesis readiness methodology, as soon as the ministry Accountable Executive (AE) has been appointed. In most instances, the AE is the COO or a clinical executive.

Process related activities begin early in Genesis readiness and are organized in time sequence. The steps are iterative and facilitate the clear understanding of the process continuum components. We begin with a process continuum orientation as an introduction to the process components of the readiness methodology. The goal of the event is to provide the MO leadership team with foundational insights into the process components and executive deliverables associated with the process aspect of Genesis readiness.

The orientation to process continuum is led by the Trinity Information Service (TIS) readiness director, in partnership with the director of nursing informatics. This two-hour event coordinated by the readiness process team, includes the Ministry Executive Team, TIS executives and corporate clinical and revenue executives (home office). This early dialogue serves to engage the hospital leaders in the why, what, when, and how of the Genesis process activities and sets a tone for collaboration within the ministry and with the MO/home office and TIS teams.

It is important to set early expectations regarding the scope of change and the importance of executive leadership to demonstrate the collaborative nature of the Genesis journey. In order to achieve the aggressive time line and the magnitude of change, the entire organization must be aligned in the journey.

The clinical/revenue readiness methodology includes executive process deliverables related specifically to their role as leaders of transformation.

A key early executive deliverable includes the development of a high-level communication plan. This plan identifies audiences, tactics, forums, timing, and responsibilities for communication. Early communication throughout the MO is crucial to creating excitement, engagement, and the momentum necessary to sustain the change process. Executive process deliverables are tracked in the detail of the clinical/revenue dashboard, and monitored throughout readiness, implementation, and post-activation optimization.

Defining the Roles

A key activity early in readiness includes the definition and selection of individuals in the ministry organization to fill key roles. This task is not unique to most EHR implementations; however, Trinity has incorporated a few nontraditional roles in our change management plan that help support our focus on process redesign. One such role is the Department Operations Expert Resource (DOER). One or two of these individuals are identified to serve as process/operational experts for each department. These frontline clinicians are critical to understanding the current state and the identification of gaps from current state to the desired future state. They work in collaboration with department leaders, informatics associates, and the readiness team. This is a fairly new role that was established in 2009 with the development of our standard delivery model. These individuals have been a key factor in the success of our process redesign.

Process liaisons also possess a key role in our methodology. These individuals are assigned to clinical departments and serve as the facilitator for the process components of Genesis readiness. This role was developed in order to provide sufficient support to clinical and revenue liaisons, DOERs and department leaders as they define their current state and seek to close gaps. These individuals are carefully selected prior to the Integrated Process Review (IPR) event held within three months of project kick-off.

The MO also identifies a service line lead for each clinical/revenue area. These are most often managers or directors. They are accountable for leadership in collaboration with the liaisons to complete required tasks in the clinical/revenue methodology.

Product Overview and Early Application Training

Product overview is conducted by the TIS training team prior to detailed discussions of process. An introduction to the Genesis clinical and revenue applications serves to prepare participants for the IPR. We have found that this early high-level system training enables users to understand the technology so they can apply this understanding to the future state when the technology is married with improved processes.

Early application training consists of more detailed system training for DOERs, liaisons, physician coaches, and physician service line champions. This additional training event enables these individuals to provide leadership for ongoing process accountabilities.

Performance Excellence Training

The magnitude of change that is required during Genesis readiness and activation requires an understanding of Performance Excellence principles. In order to achieve best practice processes, it is helpful to have key readiness team members competent in LEAN principles. Once key roles have been filled, these individuals are enrolled in Performance Excellence training sessions. The Corporate Performance Excellence Department collaborates with the ministry leaders to establish the training plan.

The plan is individualized based on the resources available and the needs of the organization. Some of our large organizations have existing Performance Excellence resources that assist or provide the education. In some instances, corporate employees serve as trainers. The goal is to enable the MO readiness team, including department leads, clinical liaisons, physician liaisons, revenue liaisons, process liaisons and DOERs, to think LEAN and to strive to create best practice processes.

This training empowers the team to question the attitude of "we've always done it that way" and to consider new or creative processes for achieving excellence in care experience, improved quality, and enhanced safety.

Integrated Process Review (IPR)

Following the Executive Process event product overview, planning begins for the Integrated Process Review (IPR). Trinity Health has developed over 250 best practice process flows. These Visio-based documents articulate the high-level integration of clinical care with the Genesis technology.

The IPR, a three- to four-day event held at the MO, involves a facilitated review of 30–35 of the 250 process flows. The selection of process flows for review is individualized based on the nuances of the hospitals' key services. The event is facilitated by the readiness process experts in partnership with subject matter clinical experts from the home office (corporate offices). The goal of the sessions is to seek to understand the organization's current state processes and identify gaps in current state compared to the desired future state, as depicted in the process flows. We also review a number of end-to-end processes including patient admission and discharge. These end-to-end processes provide clinical and revenue associates with important insights into the interdependent nature of our care processes, which create excellence in care experience. Review of department specific processes, while focused on a particular clinical area, serves to educate all departments regarding the integration of technology and clinical care.

Key physician champions are invited to segments of the event related to their specialty. In addition, HIM Patient Access, Patient Financial Services, UR/Case Management and all patient care areas are in attendance. While it may seem costly to include departments in sessions that may not directly relate to their accountabilities, it sets the stage for the partnership and learning that must occur to achieve the Genesis goals. It is well worth the expense.

The readiness process consultant facilitates the review of each flow projected on a large screen. We ask participants to let us know if their current state differs from the future state being described. We clarify our understanding of the gap and then it is recorded by the liaison staff. We also pause at key process steps that are known to be problem prone or complex. Having conducted these events at all our ministries, we have learned the areas where most ministries have issues. For example, during physician order entry, concerns about verbal order practices usually come to light. Attendees are pleased to know that they are not the only organization dealing with these issues. Again, the power of being a member of a system begins to be valued. We help participants understand that the entire system is at their disposal to address these process issues. While the event primarily serves to identify process gaps, it also serves as a training event for the MO leaders who will continue the facilitation of the remainder of the 250-plus process flows.

At the end of each day, the readiness process facilitator, director of nursing informatics, and the MO liaison team review the gaps identified during that days' process flow reviews. The purpose of gap identification is to capture the ongoing efforts aimed at closing the gaps in order to achieve the best practice processes. The gaps are scored 1 through 3 based on risk; a 1 represents high risk to the success of the implementation if not closed, while a 3 is considered low risk.

We often find that recorded gaps require education and are forwarded to the training coordinators for inclusion in future educational activities. We record all gaps identified by the participants. This is essential to honoring the culture of the current environment. Setting the tone of "seeking to understand" is a key Trinity guiding principle. On occasion, there are issues identified that may pose a practice concern. These practice concerns are categorized as such and are called out separately in the executive summary (as described in the next section).

While the purpose of the IPR is to identify gaps, it also engages associates at all levels of the organization early in the Genesis journey. We create a safe environment where associates feel comfortable sharing longstanding cultural, process, or patient safety issues. This event translates the principles of collaboration into a working model for ongoing activities and creates a culture of transparency.

IPR Executive Summary
Following the IPR event, an executive summary is created. An executive debrief is conducted on the last day prior to the team leaving. The executive summary documents the gaps identified as high risk, along with any identified practice concerns. A complete spreadsheet of all identified gaps and their risk score is embedded in the summary. The director of nursing informatics

reviews the executive summary with the genesis executive oversight team (GEOT) comprised of MO, TIS, and home office clinical executives.

The high-risk gaps are added to the clinical/revenue dashboard where their resolution is monitored. This provides excellent visibility to issues identified by frontline staff and managers. Careful tracking and regular status updates at GEOT meetings encourages sufficient attention and allocation of resources to address the closure of the high-risk gaps. Gaps that cannot be closed require an exception request to alter the best practice. In our experience, most ministries are able to achieve the best practices. Since Trinity has organizations in 10 states, we do find some required adaptation based on state regulatory variation.

IPR – Gap Analysis/Process Drill Down

Following the IPR event, the process liaisons continue the work of reviewing process flows and performing more detailed process drill downs with their assigned departments. They schedule sessions with department leads and department DOERs, including DOERs from any other department key to the process. The teams review all relevant process flows in the process manager database (PMD). There are 250 process flows in the PMD categorized by service or department so they can easily be assigned to process liaisons. The process flows in the PMD are high level and require additional drill down discussions in order to provide clarity to the process. Since we only review 30 of the 250 available process flows during the IPR, MOs spend four to six months in completing the necessary process drill down. Readiness process consultants from TIS provide support to the ministries as they complete the drill down efforts. Unified Clinical Organization (UCO), Unified Revenue Organization (URO) and TIS subject matter experts are also available for consultation. The process drill down sessions continue the model of empowering frontline caregivers in the Genesis transformation.

MOs take the standard process flows and make them their own by adding labels that individualize the process flows to their organization; however, this does not include process step changes.

Once finalized, these process flows are integrated into educational materials and are utilized in process simulation events.

Process Simulation

Process simulation is a key checkpoint in the process component of Genesis readiness. It is during process simulation that technology and process are joined. Process simulation is conducted following user validation testing (UVT), which assures that technical issues with the build are addressed prior to the integration of process testing.

During this event, trainers, super users, liaisons and department leads take part in simulating clinical scenarios. The MO, in collaboration with the TIS site analysts, develops test scripts (clinical scenarios) to simulate. These include standard scripts such as an outpatient surgery, an open heart surgery, a labor and delivery, and a pneumonia inpatient. Some ministries develop unique scripts to address unique high-volume or problem-prone processes in their organization. Support is provided to the ministry by the site analyst leads and members of the home office clinical teams. The simulation is conducted in the clinical environment and includes performing all steps in a particular patient encounter from registration through discharge. An integrated test domain is utilized and all functions are performed. Patients are registered, orders are written, tests results are posted, and care is documented. Issues are identified and recorded. We conduct multiple rounds of process simulation; at least two rounds are recommended.

Round one takes two to four weeks depending on the size of the organization. An executive summary is produced following the first round of process simulation. Debriefs are held at the end of the day and at the end of each week. In addition to the expected goals of simulation, Round 1 also serves as a training event for MO process liaisons and site analysts so that they will be able to proceed with conducting the subsequent rounds independently. The event enables process and system issues to be identified for resolution prior to activation. We always find some process issues that require change prior to activation. This significantly reduces the number and complexity of process failures at cutover. Process changes identified at process simulation are incorporated into super user and end user training materials. This aspect of readiness provides an amazing level of quality control for our planned transformation.

Go-Live Process Support

The cutover process for Genesis activation is a well-orchestrated event. A comprehensive command center is staffed at the Ministry. The command center is staffed by Trinity information services staff as well as associates from the revenue and clinical divisions of the corporate offices. The command center approach is not uncommon for a large-scale EHR implementation; however, even with all the attention to the details of the intersection of process, people, culture, and technology, there are always issues to address. Overall, we find many more process issues in the early weeks following cutover than those related to technology. During daily status meetings, process issues are reported by department leads. Resolution of department process issues is managed by the department lead and process liaisons. During the status meeting, leaders who have cross-department process issues can ask for assistance from their colleagues. A facilitator is named, a time to meet and meeting location is assigned, and the team begins its work. Progress on resolution of issues is reported daily at the status meetings in order to assure timely resolution of issues and to provide needed resources. Process excellence experts are available at activation to serve as consultants to the problem solving teams. Super users, liaisons, and physicians from all current live sites also volunteer to serve as subject matter experts during issue resolution. Associates not on site dial in to sessions when they are needed. Once the command center closes following the second week, issue resolution continues through the readiness structure of multidisciplinary teams. Collaboration becomes the way of the future.

Post-activation Review

In order to assess Genesis adoption, training, readiness methodology, and the impact of process changes, we seek feedback from our clinical users. A post-activation review is conducted within six to eight weeks following activation. This two- to three-day event consists of a series of individual and group interviews with nursing, physician, and ancillary departments. A set of interview questions is customized for each ministry organization. The interviews as facilitated by a variety of home office clinical and TIS clinical leaders. Physician interviews are held by rounding on the nursing units or physician lounges. We have had great success with obtaining feedback from physician users by utilizing existing physician forums such as grand rounds and routine medical staff department meetings.

Interview groups are customized by organization but typically include emergency departments, perinatal services, critical care, surgery and medical surgical units. ancillary meetings are conducted with lab, radiology, dietary, respiratory therapy, rehab services, and pastoral care. The interview questions focus on user perceptions of key successes, key challenges, training issues, readiness activities, and process changes. We are also very interested in the impact of Genesis on users' perception of quality, safety, efficiency, and effectiveness.

A session with members of the nursing leadership team facilitated by the corporate director of nursing informatics enables a discussion of their role in the clinical transformation. Key topics include changes to their workflow, nursing care documentation monitoring, and the impact to nursing productivity. It is important to remember that even though these leaders are not providing daily direct patient care, their work is also transformed.

One key outcome of the post-activation review is capturing lessons learned. These documents are made available to subsequent organizations in flight. It is also an aspect of our quality control and findings that are used to make changes to our readiness methodology.

A consistent theme in all MOs is the recognition that being part of a large health system has tremendous advantages. During the early weeks following cutover and implementation, the site sees the 200–300 super users from other organizations in the health system on-site, helping to support them. This may be the first time that frontline staff realizes the power of system collaboration in this very personal way. While Trinity's big-bang approach is daunting, users quickly appreciate the advantages of this approach as they experience the immediate clinical integration and system support.

The post-activation review executive summary is finalized within two weeks of the two- or three-day site visit. An executive debriefing is held prior to the team leaving. The executive summary captures a summary of the successes and opportunities, which are organized by overall themes as well as by department and role. Blinded details of all user feedback are documented in a spreadsheet that is attached to the report. Follow-up recommendations are provided when relevant. We also capture areas where users need more education. Normally by six to eight weeks, users are eager to obtain refresher education and advanced tips and tricks. This report is forwarded to the TIS training team, which utilizes the feedback to develop the enhanced education provided within three to four months post-activation. This training focuses on key problem areas and includes advanced tips and tricks for successful system use to those who are ready.

SUMMARY

Trinity has had amazing success in achieving its vision to unite state-of-the-art computer information systems with best practice clinical, revenue, and resource planning processes across the health system. We have accomplished these successes through our unrelenting focus on the four key components of creating lasting transformational change: people, process, culture, and technology. A collaborative approach includes a focus on supporting people; assuring a culture of collaboration, which improves quality and patient safety; integrating enabling technology; and paying critical attention to best practice processes. Trinity's aggressive implementation plan has been made possible through the devotion and commitment of the entire health system. I am honored to be able to tell the story of what is possible when an organization focuses on its mission, vision, and values and dares to dream big.

CONFIRMATION AND COMMITMENT
VIA A SIGN-OFF SYSTEM

We've all installed new software where you are required to scroll through a long document and at the end are forced to check the box that says, "I have read and accept these terms." You click yes, even if you didn't read the terms and have no idea what you signed. That phenomenon is the exact opposite of a sign-off system.

Once the leadership team has completed its analysis and worked out the kinks, employees and managers in every hospital, department, and floor should sign and date, on paper, their confirmation that they understand the forthcoming new work and process requirements and the need to be fully trained to prepare for their implementation. This form, depicted in Figure 4-3, should be included in your "go, no go" decision meeting with facility leadership, which is typically held two weeks prior to the projected go-live date. If you don't have a comprehensive set of accurately completed sign-off letters, it could delay a go-live date. Obtain the original and allow the facility leader to retain a copy. The end user may opt to have a copy as well.

A signed confirmation and commitment letter is essential. It ensures employees' buy-in and avoids having them claim that they didn't know the changes were coming. Individuals could be on maternity leave, extended vacation, or away from the organization for other reasons. If an employee has difficulty in completing the training because of these circumstances and is not signing off as prescribed, that individual's employment could be in jeopardy. It is important to reinforce that training is mandatory; if you don't train, you don't work.

Continually emphasize the need to practice, to receive more training, and to review the new policies. Staying current becomes a condition of continuing employment, which is no light measure.

For a single facility there will be less work administering the sign-off procedures, and it is more likely that everyone will be marching to the same drum. You would still employ this process for a single office, lab, clinic, or private practice. You might not need four weeks of lead time, and your review packet could be smaller, resulting in less work for your team. Being smaller has its advantages.

SITE READINESS

As a facility prepares for activation, that facility's entire leadership team should meet one time for a summary of how the EHR will impact

Hospital Letterhead and Logo (optional)

In preparation for the electronic health record (EHR) go-live, I understand that I must attend and satisfactorily complete all required technology training prior to EHR activation. If I do not complete this training, I will not be scheduled to work until I do so. I further acknowledge the following:

1. I will be scheduled for training and I will treat each training shift as a regularly scheduled shift. Sick calls and absences will be handled the same as regularly scheduled shifts. Time and attendance policies apply.

2. Vacations will be limited during the training months. I understand that vacations and absences will be granted on a case-by-case basis.

3. All roles accessing the EHR will be required to take Web-based training. This training must be completed prior to classroom training.

4. All roles documenting in the EHR will be required to take classroom training.

5. Management has made a commitment to provide the support I need to complete my training. Should I have any concerns, questions, or issues I will report these to my manager.

In signing, I am committed to completing the required training so that I am fully trained and prepared for the EHR activation.

Employee: _____   Date: _____

Figure 4-3: Sample Commitment Letter

each department. The future states of workflow processes should be presented to the leadership team led by their facility champions. A packet needs to be prepared for them describing those processes that will start, those that will stop, and those that will continue.

Encourage participants to read the packet in advance. Whether or not they do so, every new process is covered outlining which activities will end, start, or continue. Reviewing the entire packet, with everyone on the leadership team present, serves as a facility-level method to gain leadership buy-in and work out any kinks.

These facility leadership meetings represent the icing on the cake: representatives from every department have already been through weeks of workflow sessions. These meetings offer the chance to see the whole system at work before the facility has to use it and to solidify the future state processes in the minds of the attendees.

Post the entire packet on your intranet, complete with a user-friendly index. This packet will prove to be highly useful during activations. If a user contacts a member of your team at the command center with a question on how to handle a particular process, refer such inquirers to the file online and walk the user through it.

Each call received is a huge opportunity to reinforce the system design. You can never count on everyone remembering how to do everything. Knowing that users have easy access to the information online and that they can call you, or ask any super user, at any time is reassuring.

Transformation Management Roadmaps
A large implementation has many moving parts, and it can be overwhelming for facility leadership to know what is happening at any given time as the implementation draws nearer. A roadmap approach visually displays deliverables and events by focus areas such as *training, physician readiness, activation,* and *communication* that are on the path to activation for each facility. Facility leadership can use this type of roadmap to help visualize the engagement plan and prepare their teams for upcoming activities.

Intermittent Reinforcement
To reinforce what users can expect, offer them charts with time lines in printed packets and online. Encourage the super users and physician champions to explain things in meetings with staff, physicians, and entire departments. Encourage anyone with knowledge of how the system works to share his or her knowledge with others.

Cart Tours
To be extra sure that end users receive the reinforcement needed to make systemwide adoption a reality, use "cart tours." Outfit a rolling office cart with information about the EHR, snacks, and a flashing light. Clinical leaders and super users should wheel the cart around the floors and units.

As physicians and clinicians are working, EHR cart operators ask, "Do you know that the EHR is coming? Do you know what it can do?" Then they deliver key messages and offer important information about the forthcoming transformations.

As the cart travels throughout the departments of the hospital, everyone is encouraged to collect the information and obtain Sneak Peek preview tickets. A Sneak Peek preview is a combined event and exhibition that introduces the EHR's functionality. During a Sneak Peek preview, designated stations display presentations that highlight the new workflow and system capabilities. Other stations provide information related to transformation management, training, communications, and physician adoption. Sneak Peek previews should also be employed to encourage participants to fill out the transformation management survey discussed earlier.

To showcase and demonstrate functionality, one table or room corner where a Sneak Peek preview is held will focus on a specific department, for example the ED. Visitors to this exhibit can see all the changes forthcoming on big screens. People from that department, who were part of the design team, should staff the exhibit.

During the event, have the super users address the whole room to present a day-in-the-life, patient-centered story. This story should walk participants through precisely what happens to a patient in the new system and highlight the benefits and key messages. At each Sneak Peek preview display table, staff should be on hand to answer any questions that a physician or employee might pose. The same type of promotional items that were available at the cart tours should be available as incentives at the Sneak Peek preview.

Cart tours and the ensuing Sneak Peek previews should occur about two months before a go-live date. Paying homage to Kotter's methodology, create a sense of urgency about the new system.

Like Paul Revere riding through the streets of Concord, spread the word about what's coming.

INSIGHTS AND LESSONS LEARNED

- The key to transformation is constant focus on leadership, effective governance, and frontline engagement.
- To make the project a success, ensure that all employees have a role to play. When everyone knows they have a role to play and that others are counting on them, you increase the odds that everyone will do what has been asked of them.
- Establish an Organizational Transformation Team to lead your efforts; this helps establish a culture of readiness, as well as urgency.
- Create a site readiness program whereby every new process is reviewed, outlining the activities that will end, start, or continue.
- Have all managers and employees sign and date a document authentically affirming that they understand how their job will be impacted to solidify the level of commitment and to avoid claims that "I wasn't informed," or "This wasn't covered."
- Be sure to focus on physicians as part of your readiness activities. Using a tool such as a stakeholder matrix helps to identify and target the physicians with whom you will need to work closely.

THINKING FORWARD

1. Do you have a physician adoption strategy ready?
2. Do employees and team members understand the transformations coming with the EHR?
3. Do you have a manager focused on organizational transformation management for your EHR implementation?
4. Is a comprehensive stakeholder readiness assessment survey prepared for regular dissemination?
5. Do you have a team assembled to assess current state workflow? Do they understand the importance of their mission?

CHAPTER 5

Attracting and Nurturing Super Users

INTRODUCTION

The adoption of a multiphase EHR system provides an excellent illustration of the importance of the "people" aspect of transformational change. Among the variety of strategies you will employ for engaging end users, one of the most powerful is developing a Super User Program to help clinicians adapt to new and redesigned processes.

In some industries, super users might be called advocates, bird dogs, coaches, or champions. The name is not as vital as the function. They continually help others by communicating the right messages, serving as role models, and keeping progress on an upward trajectory.

FACILITY RECEPTIVITY

While many transformation leaders recognize the important role that super users play in helping others succeed, managers often do not consider the importance of establishing a well-planned Super User Program. Doing so extends beyond ensuring that a few individuals become experts in system use. These critical clinicians have to own the system and look for ways to continually improve it, then communicate these improvement opportunities back up through appropriate governance groups for evaluation in the EHR enhancement process. Thus, their role never ends.

To begin this process, you should address such questions as:
- Is there buy-in from the leaders in your organization?
- Is there a plan for selecting super users?
- What will the program cost and who will pay for it?

- How will super users be managed and who will manage them?

Laying out a strategy and having these topics discussed and approved at a leadership level up front helps drive success and ongoing adoption.

A PLANNED AND INTENTIONAL APPROACH

Every step of the super user process needs to be planned and intentional if you want the program to take hold. Creating a document that summarizes the Super User Program and explains its purpose, scope, and functionality is vital. As with any organizational transformation process, it all comes down to getting the appropriate leadership to sign off on what you want to do and how you want to do it. The length of the document is irrelevant—you can produce a general statement or a detailed plan. What's important is that you create a written guide so as to avoid ambiguity and achieve buy-in from both leadership and stakeholders.

Key Elements to Include

Purpose and Background: This section contains a statement of the goal of the Super User Program as well as some general information on the project, such as why it's necessary and what it will accomplish.

Program Summary and Scope: The summary includes a definition of the super user, a review of how the program is organized, the rationale for the super user model, and a list of factors that are critical to the success of the program. The scope could include assumptions about the program, its objectives and benefits, and relevant risk management strategies.

Roles and Responsibilities: Cite who is doing what, at what times, for what reasons. Create a table as depicted in Table 5-1 that details the responsibilities, the amount of training, and the approximate number of hours that will be spent per month/week/day for each super user. Many organizations do not lay this information out in such detail; however, doing so clarifies the expectations of all individuals involved and can be beneficial in the planning process.

Program Organization: This section includes the specifics of the program, such as how super users will be selected, recruited, and retained; the numbers needed and the amount of time involved; an overview of training activities; and a list of ongoing super user activities.

Duties	Time Commitments
Ensure that all users are signed up for training	8 months pre-activation = 1–3 hours/month
Assist end users with remediation training and practice	
Ensure assigned areas understand downtime procedures	4 months pre-activation = 5–10 hours/week
Proctor classroom training and maintain familiarity with service desk escalation and downtime procedures	
Provide support to end users	2 months pre-activation = 10–15 hours/week
Analyze work habits, processes, and system use by end users	
Complete monthly quality checks	Activation: 8–12 hours/day (one per shift)
Attend super user meetings post activation and disseminate information	
Facilitate filtering and prioritization of local enhancement requests post activation	Post-activation: 2–4 hours/month

Table 5-1: Super User Program Duties and Time Commitments

How Many Super Users?

Hold regular meetings with your super users to keep communication lines open before, during, and after go-live events. Super users serve as a conduit for both sending and receiving information throughout the operational departments of the health system, thus providing valuable feedback and avoiding communication issues. However, no single method of determining the essential number of super users for each department or clinical unit exists. Consider the level of impact the transformation will have and the specific functionality being implemented, and align that information with your available budget for your Super User Program.

You should arrive at estimated numbers by both polling other healthcare organizations that are implementing similar systems and functionality and by collaborating with the finance department. Create a calculation tool that encompasses the number of departments, the number of shifts, the hours of operation, the hours per shift, and the number of days supporting activation.

When contemplating the number of super users, keep in mind that this mini workforce requires management. If you are implementing considerable functionality and new processes at once, consider establishing a "lead super user," similar to the role of a charge nurse. Depending on the size of the facility, the lead super user might constitute a full-time position during an activation period and a part-time position post-activation. In a smaller facility, a manager could serve as your lead super user. In any setting, it's essential to identify an individual who can dedicate time and is willing to take on this responsibility.

If a facility appears to be short on super users, urge them to add to their ranks and help them determine what number they need. Explain and reinforce the benefits of having super users in ensuring a successful go-live, as well as sustaining the change after go-live and facilitating ongoing enhancements.

Planning each step of a Super User Program in detail may seem daunting, but the results are worth the effort. Without rigorous planning, it's unlikely that a Super User Program can be successful.

IDENTIFYING POTENTIAL SUPER USERS

Super users have a way of finding you, often before you find them. Nevertheless, having a process in place for super user recruitment is essential. Work with the leadership teams in your facilities and across various departments to explain what makes a good super user. Also, have an established program to help super users understand their vital role in the project. Discuss the purpose and background of the Super User Program, their specific roles and responsibilities, and the time commitment involved. Those who wish to proceed should attend an orientation program. You should also consider having them and their manager sign a letter of commitment. It's important to spell out the time commitment details and to have a clear understanding up front.

Ask facilities if they need help in selecting super users, but allow each facility to develop its own individual selection criteria and its own method of administering the program. Some hospitals might have a clinical ladder for super users. Some pay super users a little extra for their efforts. Lay the groundwork for facilities to hold ongoing super user meetings, and explain their importance.

Characteristics of a Super User

Don't assume that computer skills are all that's needed to become a super user. The role also requires strong communication skills to be able to answer questions from end users and to assist with end-user adoption during and after activation, as well as ongoing optimization activities. Additionally, super users should receive training on how to deal with resistance, so having some skills in conflict resolution as a

Super User Characteristics	
Consistently display strong values	Understand how current initiatives enhance long term goals
Maintain a strong sense of responsibility and project commitment	Have a demonstrated history of supporting others
Motivate others	Possess a people orientation with sound interpersonal skills
Train others effectively	Understand workflow processes
Handle and reduce potential resistance	Possess analytical and problem solving skills
Serve as a mentor and coach	Have experience with computers

Table 5-2: Snapshot of a Super User

baseline that can be developed through training is also very important. Table 5-2 depicts characteristics of a super user that are both important and helpful when requesting managers to identify super users.

Super users serve as a facility's frontline support assisting with clinical workflow and system utilization. Hence, super users play a pivotal role on the path to system adoption. Moreover, activation is not an endpoint for super users. It is the beginning of a role that will continue indefinitely. This point cannot be overemphasized. EHR implemenation is just the beginning. There will always be enhancements, optimization, and new functionality long after a system is implemented. Super users will be needed to maintain the transformation and assist with adoption of new tools and functionality.

Super-User Training Program

Training those who have been carefully selected to be super users comes next. A good super user training program employs several elements. Besides completing basic end-user training, super users need to receive advanced instruction, such as "Tips & Tricks" training. Every super user should receive this in-depth training, typically lasting one to two days depending on the complexity of the EHR functionality being implemented. "Tips & Tricks" training covers issues that typically frustrate or confound end users, reviews the activation support model, and includes methods for navigating the system and handling resistance.

The last component of the super user training program is practice. Super users need to practice a few hours per week and have the opportunity to apply the training they've received. Follow up with your super users and make sure they are practicing. Accountability is critical; don't just assume it will happen.

When a facility is ready to go-live, having super users on hand is crucial. In the weeks leading up to activation, super users play an extensive role, often spending long hours helping in every way possible. Give them a checklist of topics each and every day, as well as key workflows to review with clinicians and physicians before go-live as they round. This process of "readiness rounds" is very valuable in terms of reinforcing key future state workflows. After go-live, provide each facility with the tools its super users need to remain up to date.

CONTINUED SUPPORT

Training is what makes a super user super, but it's not the end of the process. Becoming a super user is a long-term commitment. As with physicians, track the activity of super users. Just as you give special attention to physicians because of the business they bring to your organization, give special attention to super users because they represent your internal advocates and operational champions.

Super users are the ambassadors for the new system and will continue to support its operation for years to come. They must maintain relationships with everyone in the facility who is connected to the system. This includes all end users: physicians, service desk staff, IT, project team members, and facility leadership.

Regardless of the methods chosen, it is highly beneficial to keep super users engaged and in the loop before, during, and after activation. After go-live, consider having annual performance goals for super users to keep them involved and focused.

After an implementation phase ends, super users are essential for "hardwiring" the new processes and workflow that have been implemented. After all, a go-live activation date is merely a point in time. What happens afterwards spells the difference between a project's success or failure.

An EHR is not stagnant; changes and improvements will occur on an ongoing basis. Super users are critical in terms of offering vital information and updates to clinicians and physicians about what is happening with the system.

Starting the Engine

While hospitals may have variations on the theme of super users, all strong programs have the same key components. Super users represent the gasoline and motor oil that allow the engine to run at peak performance. The project manager and implementation team simply can't be everywhere. An EHR implementation is a project with a beginning and an end. During the interim and thereafter, the nurses, physicians, IT staff, administrative staff, and other ancillary team members own it. They've got to support each other to make it vibrant and to constantly improve usability.

SUMMARY

Implementing a Super User Program involves planning extensively, developing selection criteria to identify the most qualified individuals, creating a training program that prepares super users to become experts, and nurturing them for long-term involvement in the EHR's evolution. If carried out properly, such efforts will shorten the end user's learning curve, provide support for problem resolution at the point of need, create a feedback mechanism that will facilitate improvements to future training and deployment, and encourage continued growth in system use and functionality over time.

INSIGHTS AND LESSONS LEARNED

- Buy-in from a facility's leadership is fundamental for a Super User Program to succeed.
- Create a document that summarizes the Super User Program and explains its purpose, scope, and organization so that there is a clear understanding of the program across the organization.
- Determining the essential number of super users for each department or clinical unit can be challenging. It needs to be based on what is being implemented, who is affected, and how much of an organizational change will occur.
- Super users should practice a few hours per week prior to go-live and stay current about system updates; there is no margin for coasting.

- If executed properly, a Super User Program will shorten the end user's learning curve, provide quick problem resolution, and generate feedback that can improve future training and functionality.
- Super users do not go away after go-live; their ongoing role is essential to hardwiring the change as well as improving the system to make it easier and better for the clinicians and physicians.

THINKING FORWARD

1. Do you have a super users selection process for each facility?
2. Is there a career plan for the super users?
3. Is there a budget for running the program at the facility level?
4. What does your training program look like for your super users?
5. What is your plan for "super user" engagement post-activation?

CHAPTER 6

Training

INTRODUCTION

As you complete your system design, you should establish a solid training program and a detailed *training approach document* with an *executive level summary*. This document should operationalize the executive level summary and provide guidance and direction for the training team. Present the document to the senior leadership team and discuss in advance exactly what is involved in helping the clinicians and physicians learn the new system and secure leadership buy-in.

Investing in training is a crucial success factor. Without it, you would have powerful software, extensive capabilities, and illustrious plans that go nowhere. It's like having an expensive car in your driveway with all the features and benefits you've always wanted, but with no key to the ignition.

IRREFUTABLE EVIDENCE

The training *executive level summary* outlines critical success factors, and foremost among them is that physician participation in the project will be a key focus of your training efforts. If you simply told the senior leadership team that "physicians need a lot of training," the response would not be so positive. Complaints would arise that too much was being asked of physicians, that they wouldn't have the time, and that they wouldn't be agreeable.

To convince physicians and clinicians that the training levels are reasonable and necessary, collect benchmark data and include them in the executive summary. To derive benchmark data, speak to training managers in a wide variety of settings, and specifically query them about their best practices—what worked and why.

It's easy to fall into traps such as assuming that your senior management team knows what you're doing, understands your needs, and will support you at critical junctures. Relying on the assumption that physician training is not crucial because "they will pick it up as they go" is an enormous mistake. Training for physicians in the electronic world of CPOE must be mandatory if you want to be successful, and your leadership must stand behind this. Armed with reliable data, present your case to senior leaders with real-world examples of requisite training levels based on comparable project experiences at other organizations. There is often concern from physicians over the amount of training required, so if you can show some benchmark data and explain why the amount and type of training is necessary, you will get the leadership backing you need to implement a successful training program.

Once you get leadership approval and your training program established, getting non-employed physicians to sit through four- or six-plus hours of training can be a challenge. Create a sense of competition; post the names and dates of physicians who have completed training in a public area, such as the physician lounge. You will be amazed at what a little competition can do to motivate others into completing their training.

A DIFFERENT KIND OF APPROACH

As part of the project management team, you are so invested in the software and technology that you don't always think the way the end user will think. Thus, it's important to enroll the end users early and have them "test drive" the training curriculum and materials. Strive to gain some level of end-user acceptance in the training test phase *before* you deploy the system upon the masses.

Ultimately, the training approach should include a departure from what some organizations tend to do. Take an approach called "a day in the life," as in "a day in the life of a bedside clinician or physician." First, in a classroom setting, trainees finish web-based training that teaches them the basic point-and-click operations they need to know. Then, offer them a workflow-based scenario and walk them through it to give them a hands-on feel for the future state of the workflows, new processes, and the specific way to use the system. Engage your super users and physician champions from all departments to help develop these scenarios, which should be based on real-life examples of the future state workflows.

With the ability to focus in a separate room away from patients, provide them with an operation simulation environment. They can put their hands on the tools and levers of the system to give them an idea of what it would actually look like in practice. They can ask questions, make mistakes, and receive on-the-spot guidance.

Once trainees have reached a certain level of proficiency, they should complete a competency assessment to determine if they have acquired the basic core competencies to do their work in the future state. An instructor should check them off and ensure that they are able to deftly proceed down the list. For example, physicians should walk away from CPOE training knowing how to enter a complex order, such as sliding scale insulin. Nurses should know how to document vital signs and medications. It's important that your instructors make sure clinicians know how to operate and function with some of the core competencies in the future state.

Trainees typically don't remember all of what they were taught. Too often, the expectation following training is that enrollees now know everything needed to do the job. Instead, deliver the message: When you've finished the classroom training, you will have developed some core competencies, but the training does not end. You need to have hands-on practice for the lessons to take hold. What's more, you have to carve out time from your normal schedule to master the system. Person by person, everyone needs to devote extra time and effort. It's important that you get management to understand this so they can provide accountability for practice. The bottom line is this: if end users practice, it will make their go-live smoother.

Full Immersion

Trainees should have a six- to eight-week window of opportunity to fully immerse themselves in the system, learn the new procedures, master the point-and-click aspects of entering data, and deftly navigate the system before the go-live activation date for their facility. Training more than six to eight weeks in advance is too far out from the go-live date, and they will not remember what they have learned. Ensure that they have time to revisit the workflow scenarios presented and intently practice what they have been taught. Post the workflow scenarios on the intranet or give them a copy to take with them so they can do this.

Give them a list of where they might find job aids and specific guidelines, as well as all of the new policies and procedures. Arm them as expertly as possible with training packets acting as boiled-down sets of instructions that they can use as quick references at their stations, such as "five ways to accomplish this" and "four tips to handle that."

With super users embedded in all departments and in reasonably close proximity to all trainees, you will have a virtual army of on-the-spot supporters, encouragers, and trail guides in place.

READINESS ROUNDS

As part of training, provide what are called *readiness rounds*. Have the super users, as well as physician champions and other people on the project team, make the rounds through the facilities. They should discuss some of the key training topics and demonstrate some of the key training points, including "tips and tricks," all before the go-live date. In essence, you're not showing up on a go-live day and saying, "Okay, bingo! Your system is live." You're partnering with the super users and optimizing their value and services.

Much like a countdown in the control room at the Kennedy Space Center, prepare your crews so that lift-off has the highest chance of succeeding. Prepare a checklist of topics for readiness rounds so that your super users and physician champions are aware of what needs to be covered four, three, two, and even one week prior to go-live.

Despite all the planning and preparation and all the activities and assistance provided, things can still go wrong. Resistance can arise at any time, and people can feel anxious. A small percentage of clinicians will represent problems. Others may be fearful that they will be unable to switch over to the new system.

Just as the major airlines have programs for nervous fliers, your super users should be trained to help nervous or reluctant end users handle issues in advance of their potential occurrence. Provide classes for the super users specifically on dealing with resistance. The class topics can vary widely, including "How to deal with an angry physician," "How to deal with a nurse who doesn't want to use the system," and "How to handle a user who blanks out and can't even get started."

The sum of these activities yields a level of friendly indoctrination that can notably impact the culture. Becoming an advocate of the new system is *de rigueur*. If you're still resistant weeks before go-live, you run the risk of being regarded as dead weight. Strive to imbue the feeling that the changeover will be beneficial systemwide, for everyone, so why not hop aboard?

THE HUMAN ELEMENT

Within large health systems, experiences can vary widely from facility to facility. If your system consists of one hospital, some of this complexity may not be an issue. However, you will encounter some variation between departments and some difficulty with specific individuals. If you have a senior executive at one hospital who's not walking the walk, it trickles down to all levels of staff.

What a wonderful world it would be if everyone simply bought into the project at the outset. Alas, you'll encounter some human obstacles who will need a bit of extra attention and care. Resistance can come from anyone, including executives. It's important to develop a plan to deal with resistance even at the executive level. It's often effective to meet with those key leaders who might be a bit resistant to new ways of operating, and review all the positive developments occurring as well as future benefits. Out of sight to others, provide one-on-one coaching at the executive level.

For example, an executive at one facilty once announced: "I don't want to lead any activation committees." The project team reminded this leader that other leaders, in similar roles at similar facilities, had successfully come on board and led activation committees. With this bit of peer pressure, he began to succomb. The team reminded him: "You are so passionate about your staff. You have their hearts and they will follow you. They will do whatever you want and we will do whatever it takes."

Call it benign manipulation if you want, but here is where the project leaders and project teams earned their paychecks. By objectively conveying the situation to the executive, referring back to his counterparts, and using his terminology, his resistance softened a little. In time, he came aboard. This example illustrates that resistance emerges in settings of all sizes. Not everyone wants to lead or be a part of massive organizational transformation.

We each arrive at our current career positions with various experiences, aims, and inclinations. Each person you encounter has a different background, education, and training. You can't always determine who's going to be an advocate and who's going to be a resister. As the old adage goes, management would be easy if it weren't for the human element.

STRUCTURE AND RESOURCES

Understandably, one of the key hurdles for a smaller healthcare system is funding. Some organizations don't devote the resources required to provide effective training vital to the success of the project. What can smaller facilities, with fewer resources, do? Most importantly, they must *leverage their resources.*

Virtually every organization has unidentified trainers within. Identify staff members who are already adept at training and recruit them, even if their training experience is from another discipline. For example, the clinical educators you employ are trainers. They can apply the tools and training techniques they've developed throughout their careers in the context of your transformation management initiative. Leverage their skills and abilities so they become effective in teaching others the new system.

It's easier to work with people already employed by your system, and who are already good at training, and "retool" them. It is harder to make trainers out of people who are effective with EHRs but who are not adept at training others.

People already on board in your hospital who are not super users or even trainers might also serve as trainers for you. Such people have been trained in the system and display an affinity for it. Perhaps with your help, they now realize that they can serve as trainers themselves. Be on the lookout for such people. Announce your desire to recruit from within.

Let it be known, systemwide, that everyone who has the inclination or even suspects that they could be a competent trainer may apply.

In the early days of a project it may be difficult to find skilled labor and skilled analysts locally. Faced with few options, you may need to grow and develop the people you have. Hiring clinicians, nurses, and especially those with intensive care or ED skills who typically possess strong technical skills can prove to be some of the best talent to serve as trainers. Such nurses have potential, as well, for becoming system analysts, and hiring them as trainers is a good place to start the transformation. Invest in them considerably, and the venture will pay off.

They will be among your most consistent and effective trainers, system analysts, and system support staff.

University Ties

Much of the training that occurs during huge change management projects, particularly with physician training, is not going to happen in the classroom. You'll find it difficult to induce community physicians to sit down for four hours at a time. In some cases, you'll need to draw upon every resource you can muster, including those you already have on board and students from medical schools and universities who prove effective in working one-on-one.

Your facility is likely to have relationships with local universities and community colleges. Identify, attract, and recruit students who are majoring in information science, computer science, or some other type of informatics. Employ students in this capacity at entry-level positions.

Approach a local community college with a Healthcare Informatics program and recruit students who seek to work side-by-side with seasoned healthcare professionals as trainers and providers of activation support. Teach the students the basics of the software application and processes. From there, they can serve as training and activation support staff, often providing one-on-one assistance to physicians and clinical staff. This model has proven to be very successful.

The services of a professional training firm can run from $75 to $150 per hour. On the other hand, you'll be able to work effectively with students from a nearby community college who are happy to receive $11 or $12 per hour. Train them and help them to grow. They will receive real-world experience and build their resumes and, in return, offer you real value.

A Hiring Window of Opportunity

Unemployment has been a challenging issue recently, and you may be able to leverage the economic downturn to round out your staff. For a reasonable hourly rate there is the potential to find a highly competent, experienced support staff that appreciates the opportunity to earn some short-term income.

An amazing amount of talent is available right now. Many in this talent pool are resigned, for the time being, to earning whatever they can, even at a lower hourly rate than they've previously attained. This factor varies, of course, from city to city and from state to state as unemployment and cost of living levels must be factored into these entry-level position wage rates. Nonetheless, there is a window of opportunity to pursue for securing needed support staff and providing valuable experience to those who would welcome it. Many have considerable IT experience, and although it may not necessarily be in healthcare, it's not a huge leap for them to become acclimated.

Vendor Opportunities

Your vendors represent potential training resources. Software vendors or other system-related vendors have talented staff on board. Your vendors won't farm out such people for free. So, as part of your contracts with them, negotiate a special rate, at least for some of their junior entry-level staff, to be part of your on-site training team. It's best to work with your vendor up front on such issues. Even retroactively negotiated, you don't know what kind of arrangement you can establish until you make the attempt.

Software vendors might possess a variety of prefabricated educational materials that come with their system. In an up-front arrangement, they might be able to offer this content as part of an overall package. You can then recycle that content and customize it to your needs.

CASE STUDY:
MEETING THE TRAINING CHALLENGE IN
A SMALL RURAL COMMUNITY HOSPITAL

By Sara Shultz, MS, RN-BC, CCRN, Clinical Informatics Coordinator, St. Joseph Hospital, Kokomo, Indiana

INTRODUCTION

St. Joseph Hospital, located in semi-rural north central Indiana, is an acute care hospital with 167 licensed beds serving a wide variety of patients. In addition to our acute care hospital, we also care for patients via our ambulance service in several ambulatory family practice and specialty physician clinics; home care; behavioral health; outpatient surgery; cardiopulmonary rehab; physical, occupational, and speech therapy; and two urgent care clinics. St. Joseph Hospital is part of St. Vincent Health, a system with 20 hospitals throughout Indiana, and part of Ascension Health, the largest Catholic and non-profit healthcare system in the United States. St. Joseph is accredited by The Joint Commission and is designated as a Stroke Center of Excellence by The Joint Commission. Seven hundred-fifty babies were born at St. Joseph in 2011, and the ED sees more than 35,000 patients annually.

A few years ago, we began our journey to progress from paper processes to an EHR. The initial commitment by the executive leadership team to plan for two FTEs for planning, training, and implementation demonstrates their recognition of the importance of this project. As a community hospital, our management and administration teams are very "lean." While larger hospitals might have teams of educators, project staff, and middle management that might be able to cross over and accept more of the responsibilities of an EHR implementation, our leaders recognized that our hospital did not have staff to flex into this role while still maintaining their other responsibilities.

Not surprisingly, the initiative to begin our EHR planning and implementation was met by clinical staff with both apprehension and excitement. Prior to implementing any part of our EHR, we asked clinical staff to fill out self-assessments revealing their comfort level with computer functions such as minimizing and maximizing windows, using drop-down menus, and choosing the appropriate mouse button to click. Realizing that the majority of the staff members ranked themselves as "uncomfortable" or "very uncomfortable" with basic computer functions, the clinical informaticists (both prior staff nurses at this hospital) recommended and received executive support for basic computer skills classes prior to any introduction of EHR training. From the results of the survey, we realized that though the majority of clinicians requested more technological support, there was a definite subset of very technologically savvy clinicians who were already comfortable and competent with basic computer skills. To address that disparity, we provided clinicians the option to enroll in a slower- or quicker-paced class that covered computer basics, focusing on terminology, functions, and the hospital-based email system.

This basic computer and email training prepared clinicians to be comfortable learning even more about technology when we began our EHR training. We are still in the process of implementing various aspects of our EHR, with training and implementation about every 12 months. Our EHR training was workflow based, focusing on scenarios applicable to the clinicians' daily work. The clinical informaticists realized there were many clinical areas that had processes with which we were unfamiliar, such as the birthing center, ED, and periop. We spent hours interviewing and shadowing nurses, therapists, physicians, pharmacists, and other clinicians in clinical areas less familiar to us. We were determined to apply the technical information to each clinician's framework of reference during training. Knowing that some of our staff were still anxious about using technology, we gave them the opportunity to schedule themselves in a slower-paced class that covered the same content but allowed more time and was staffed with more super users. We made a practice computer available on every nursing unit and clinical department for clinicians to practice in the training database between training and activation. We provided real-life scenarios and corresponding exercises for staff to complete on their own time and at their own pace. We also used real charts to derive training and practice scenarios and examples.

Training scheduling provides unique challenges and opportunities for a hospital of our size. While sometimes staff were not able to attend training as planned due to a clinical or staffing crisis, in other cases we were able to consolidate training by getting an entire department (such as pastoral care or case management) in the training room simultaneously. Being able to train an entire department at one time gives great consistency and opportunity for questions to be answered collaboratively.

Starting with our very first EHR training, we have partnered with our community college and local university in a new way. We invited nursing clinical instructors to participate in EHR training alongside our staff nurses, and 100 percent of the nursing instructors took advantage of this. Going forward, new instructors who will be teaching nursing clinicals at our hospital attend our new associate EHR training class. The nursing instructors then teach their clinical students how to use our EHR. We have made our training database and training classrooms and materials available to them in order to provide the most realistic and convenient training tools and environment. This not only strengthens our commitment to our partner college and university, but we are sending a very consistent message to all students and faculty, as well as our own clinicians.

We generated excitement for training by creating a large display in the hospital cafeteria and updated it with each clinician's name as he or she successfully completed an EHR class. Making each individual's training status public created anticipation and a sense of accomplishment. To carry through the thread of our executive support, we created and showed a 5-minute film at the beginning of each EHR class. The film featured our executive leaders welcoming staff to class, thanking them for their attendance and attention, and explaining how the EHR training that staff would receive that day will help our hospital meet its safety, organizational, and financial goals.

Though a community-sized hospital faces distinct challenges in EHR training related to resources (staff to backfill clinicians in training, educators, training rooms, etc.), these same principles of successful EHR implementation can be adjusted for any situation. Being aware of hospital and community resources is paramount to maximizing training potential and results. Specific roles, environment, and training plans will vary, but by carefully assessing your learners' needs, seeking out ways to creatively train for use of new technology within your established process paradigm, and following through with the philosophies in this chapter, you can achieve successful EHR training.

EMPOWER YOUR MIDDLE MANAGERS

For whatever training programs you devise, consider the impact on your middle managers—not simply the end users, but the general rank and file. The middle managers will be held responsible for ensuring the new processes and workflows take hold at the bedside, and for subsequent audits. They have the formal responsibility to ensure that end users employ the system as designed.

In one organization, approximately 200 nurse managers from across the healthcare system were assembled for the first time in the history of that health system. The project team discussed the forthcoming transformation and what their new responsibilities would be, emphasizing the important role they played in ensuring that nurses and clinicians employed the system as designed.

At the gathering, CNOs delivered key messages. Then the team distributed a manager toolkit, as depicted in Figure 6-1, that included checklists of the daily reports they would be required to audit to ensure the nurses were using the system correctly. Step by step, the team walked the nurse managers through the gamut of their new responsibilities: "This is what you need to do the first week that we go live, the second week, and so on." Most participants agreed that the toolkit was quite helpful. Put someone in your organization in charge of developing this toolkit as well as maintaining it, and post it on the intranet.

Previously in their careers, when they needed to remain organized, check their work, or audit operations, these managers referred to paper records. Now, they are learning to use the computer and the EHR to monitor patient care activities and the quality of care being delivered. With the paper trails, if something was done incorrectly, a long time could pass before someone found the problem. With greater system transparency, if something has been done incorrectly it's easier to identify the mistake.

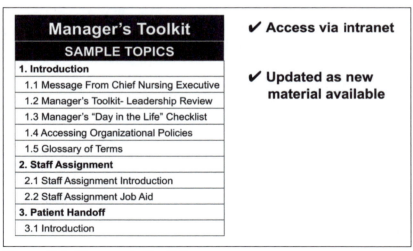

Figure 6-1: Manager's Toolkit

Chart Check: Compliance Checklist

Documentation Element	Location in EHR	Frequency of Chart Check	Date/Time Chart Reviewed	Complete
Verbal/telephone orders co-signed by physician	Check for icon on order profile	Daily		☐ Yes ☐ No
Intake and output balance	Verify all fluids were documented in I & O	Daily		☐ Yes ☐ No
Overdue tasks	Overdue Task Report	Once a shift		☐ Yes ☐ No
Lines, tubes, drains or skin breakdown present on admission (POA)	Assessment	Following admission, check daily for new admissions		☐ Yes ☐ No
Assessment	Documents	Upon admission		☐ Yes ☐ No

✔ **Can be completed by:**
- **employee**
- **super user**
- **manager**

Figure 6-2: Checklist for Monitoring Compliance with Documentation

With any automated system, problems can occur, often because of user-related issues. One can select the wrong patient or enter data incorrectly. Problems might occur at even faster speeds in an automated system, but you have an enhanced ability to examine what's transpired before something gets out of hand.

To avoid information overkill, judiciously dispense information at timed intervals. Make sure not to inundate managers while constantly monitoring their ability to absorb the information. Middle managers should be encouraged to ask questions about any elements within the toolkit. Ask, "Have you run this report today?" and "Have you completed this segment?" The goal is to help them do their jobs, but in a new, different, and ultimately more effective way. An example of a manager toolkit checklist for auditing compliance is shown in Figure 6-2.

ROLLING SUPER USERS

If you have a large health system, say, more than one or two facilities, take a subset of your super users and create "rolling super users" who can serve as a core base through all of your rollouts. Rolling super users are those who continue to develop their "super powers" and float from facility to facility during each go-live, serving as a constant source of expertise from hospital to hosptial. Unlike local super users who only work and support at their own facility, these rolling super users serve at each activation and become an army of experts that the local super users can leverage for support. They also will help with minimizing variation in processes from facility to facility and are helpful in bringing these variations to the surface for resolution when they arise.

They've done all of the basic training, as well as the super-user training. Beyond that, periodically bring this select group back for a couple days of intensive, highly focused training. This extra training reinforces what they've already learned and offers greater detail on some specific issues.

Invite rolling super user participants to attend additional hours of extra, intense system training. This may be 40-plus hours of additional training depending on the functionality being implemented. That's a lot, but some relish the opportunity. Require them to participate in every activation as they will be leaders during those times, having been through several activations already. Have these rolling super users lead "huddles" at each activation, where they help the local super users troubleshoot issues that they have dealt with before.

MEASUREMENT AND FEEDBACK

At the conclusion of each training class, collect surveys that yield revealing data. You will want to know, for instance, if the training program met users' needs. Ask about the training program's strengths and weaknesses, and allow users to rate the training based on numerous criteria.

Collect all of that information and make changes to your training curriculum, where appropriate. Deal one-on-one with problems related to a particular instructor. Assemble aggregate findings and present them to the current users before going to the next facility.

At the next facility, exhibit the ratings from your previous training programs. Why? In part, you will minimize any potential resistance. You can tell the next facility, for example, that on a scale from 1 to 5, your training program was last rated at 4.2. You want to avoid situations in which a few negative voices might prove to be the loudest. If most people are content, then your training program, undoubtedly, has considerable merit.

Each time, measure and report your training results to the next facility slated for activation. Your goal is to continually improve the training, and this allows you to demonstrate, based on the surveys, that it has improved over time.

INSIGHTS AND LESSONS LEARNED

- Powerful software, extensive capabilities, and detailed plans are useless unless you establish a solid training approach and a commensurate training approach document.
- To derive benchmark data, examine other health systems that have implemented a similar transformation campaign and ask about their best practices. What worked and why?
- Leverage your training resources by scouting for internal training talent, such as your clinical educators. For recruiting external training talent, cast a wide net among local colleges and underemployed career professionals.
- For whatever training programs you devise, your middle managers will be held responsible for the organizational transition taking place at the bedside and for subsequent audits, so empower them.
- Seek to continually improve your training by surveying participants, absorbing their feedback, and instituting the best suggestions.

THINKING FORWARD

1. Do you have a training plan and timetable to implement it?
2. Have you assessed your support staff needs and the training required for them?
3. Have you planned for a simulation environment with all the proper equipment?
4. Is "effective management of resistance" part of your training plan?
5. Do you have a plan to engage middle management in hardwiring the transformation and giving them tools to ensure success?

CHAPTER 7

Activation and Beyond

INTRODUCTION

A go-live date, also known as *activation* or *conversion*, refers to "flip-ping the switch" and formally launching a new project phase. As you now know, a great deal of time and effort precedes an activation. This chapter outlines a methodology and approach leading up to a go-live date that encompasses defining the role of everyone who's going to be a part of the activation and includes three stages of support.

THREE STAGES OF ACTIVATION SUPPORT

Activation is a huge undertaking and a critical juncture in the project, and moving from activation support to ongoing daily operations with the new tools and processes can be overwhelming for the clinicians. Therefore, divide your activation support period into phases, gradu-ally decreasing support over a defined period of time based on metrics. In this way, you ease into independence, versus pulling the plug for go-live activation support all at once. Clinicians, as well as the project team, feel less anxious when they see metrics demonstrating success and they begin to feel confident in their new workflows, which then fosters independence and less reliance on the project team. Everyone feels more comfortable moving into ongoing support and operations if you approach your activation in this manner.

Stage 1 Support

Stage 1 relates to those activities that the project team provides imme-diately upon activation. During this stage, the project team initiates command center operations. The command center provides both a mechanism to manage and coordinate the support at the facility and a centralized location for human resources.

While the clinical and technical resources, namely, project and vendor resources, are on site in large numbers, technical issues as well as process issues are identified and dealt with on a real-time basis. Super users are assigned to each department or unit to provide "at-the-elbow" support to clinicians and physicians as they use the new EHR.

Stage 1 is a critical time and, thus, on-the-spot and at-the-elbow support is provided around the clock. Think of a pilot in a cockpit. Most of the time, the pilot is spending more time than passengers ever presume checking charts and going over details before the plane lifts off. This is done for the safety of everyone on board. Pilots, as well as flight attendants and ground crew, have a number of logs and reporting forms to fill out. Only after a series of systemwide checks and clearance from the control tower can the plane roll out to the runway.

MYRIAD PREPARATIONS

Checklists serve as disarmingly simple but effective tools in helping healthcare professionals to be at their best. *The Checklist Manifesto*, a book by Atul Gawande, MD, emphasizes the importance of the checklist.[1] It is a quality-control device. In high-pressure situations, even thoroughly trained professionals can become overwhelmed. By marking items on a checklist, healthcare professionals can prevent potential costly mistakes and even fatal medical errors.

All the preparation that facilities undertake leading up to an activation likewise contributes to a successful launch. Have a checklist that is distributed and reviewed 90 days before activation. This assures that all of the necessary steps to convert a hospital from its old system to the new EHR are followed and nothing is missed. For example, the effectiveness of this tool was demonstrated at one activation when, in the midst of all the flurry of activity, a step in bringing the electronic medication administration record (eMAR) "live" was missed. This hospital had to go-live without it for a period of several hours, which caused some confusion and turmoil.

Malcolm Gladwell, author of *The Tipping Point*, observes, "It's too easy for an otherwise competent doctor to miss a step or to forget a key question, or, in the stress and pressure of the moment, to fail to plan properly for every eventuality."[2] A command center manual serves as a compendium of checklists, indicating the level of support needed for successful activation; how to secure the time, space, location, and other requirements of assembling the team; and what steps to take in various scenarios.

If you're from a small hospital, you might be thinking, "How can we do all of this? We have a small budget. This level of preparation is daunting. Who's got that kind of time and money?" The solution is to *leverage the resources* you have in your facility. Can you identify a facility coordinator to manage these operations? You don't pay anything extra, and if you emphasize the importance of a coordinator for success with facility leadership, you should be able utilize some of that person's time.

After identifying a coordinator at each facility, ask him or her for lists of where people can park, eat, hold conferences, etc., specifying the logistics of the go-live and command center. Practically speaking, you have to identify the key human resources at each facility because there is no way your project team can have that same level of local knowledge. Leveraging local resources is vital.

A hospital's primary business is taking care of patients, and you will obviously want to avoid any disruption experienced by patients as much as possible. As a minor but telling example, you don't want the activation support team to take all of the parking spaces, leaving patients and visitors with only distant parking places. An EHR implementation at a single facility would require that same kind of attention to detail, but on a smaller scale.

Stage 2 Support

The second of the three stages is characterized by clinicians who have become more familiar with the system and more comfortable in handling what have become their new, normal, routine activities.

During Stage 2, the hospital has a reduced level of support staff. Still, users will require access to knowledgeable resources for assistance when unusual or perplexing situations arise. While the number of physical supporting staff personnel might be reduced, some support needs to be available during all shifts. Depending on how the activation is proceeding, the command center might or might not be operational.

In determining when clinicians are ready for this type of support, take a hard look at your activation metrics. For example, how many orders are being entered electronically by physicians? Is this what was expected and normal for the amount of time the system has been live? If so, show this as proof to your clinicians and physicians that they are ready for a reduced level of support. Another effective metric to demonstrate readiness for reduced support is to have a metric that measures clinician and physician comfort with using the new system independently. Have your super users complete a survey, which is posted online, in which they rate the clinicians they supported that shift on a Likert Scale and describe how much assistance the clinicians needed to complete their daily activities. Gather the data in the command center and then show your leadership team proof that they are ready to start treading on their own. This fosters confidence with the facility that they are making progress and are beginning to function independently. This helps when some on staff become emotional and overreact. For example, at one facility a nurse manager said, "My staff are falling apart; they are stressed out and can't do their work." Measuring and tracking progress during an activation can help separate fact from fiction and settle any drama that may surface. Metrics and measurement are discussed further in Chapter 8.

Stage 3 Support

Stage 3 of activation support involves gravitation toward new norms. Here, the implementation team transitions support for the facility to the super users and the production support team (IT systems and application analysts) and ensures a smooth handoff from the implementation team to the facility.

After the last local hospital steering team meeting (see next section), you should conduct a formal transition for the project and support teams, including a lessons learned session that you can take forward to your next hospital or future activation(s). By now, clinicians are comfortable and proficient with the new system, and the focus is on optimal use of the system.

With activation support in three stages, you move facilities along based on feedback and metrics until their super users can independently support them. Depending on the magnitude of transformation being implemented, the type of functionality being introduced, and the number and type of users impacted, facilities might move through these stages rapidly or more slowly over a period of a few weeks. The more work you do up front to prepare, the quicker they move through these stages.

ROLES AND RESPONSIBILITIES

It's important to spell out responsibilities and expectations in advance. For example, this chapter defines the role of the activation manager, the command center manager, the leader of a "SWAT Team" (defined later in this chapter) and so on. The idea is to leave as little to chance as possible while promoting facility ownership of the activation.

It's understandable if you feel a bit overwhelmed by the variety of groups and leaders that need to be established to aid in the activation phase. It takes a wide range of skills and talents to ensure a successful activation. The list is long, including executive sponsors, activation coordinators, activation managers, and command center managers. The types of resources needed to support an activation could include a communciation coordinator (to handle daily communication updates), a manager on call (for technical issues), an administrative assistant (to handle the dozens and dozens of phone calls and drop-ins at the command center), super users, break-fix support staff, IT service desk, and network support, as well as the IT provisioning team. The amount and type of resources you will need will be dependent upon what you are implementing and the number of clinicians impacted.

You should be prepared to plan and budget for many types of resources because an EHR implementation of this scale represents significant transformation and merits massive coordination, with everyone's roles and responsibilities clearly defined up front. If you are unsure of what you may need, network with other hospitals or healthcare organizations to get some benchmark data.

KEY GROUPS FOR INITIATING
AND RUNNING AN ACTIVATION

Local Hospital Steering Team

Comprising a group of key leaders at a hospital, this group has oversight responsibility for the activation. It consists of facility and physician leadership, as well as project leadership. This group makes key decisions, such as when to restrict system access by physicians who

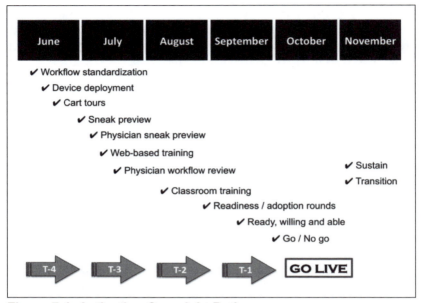

Figure 7-1: Activation Oversight Path

have not been trained, when to cut back on activation support, the go/no-go decision, and so on.

This leadership group keeps tabs on activation activities and adoption, and resolves critical issues that impact the activation. Engage this team a few months before activation so they can work through any issues ahead of time that might impede success. Figure 7-1 depicts a sample representation of the processes that this group oversees preceding an activation.

Super Users SWAT Teams

SWAT Teams ensure that the facility and the EHR project team collaborate to address and resolve process issues immediately preceding and during a go-live. The SWAT Team leader is identified and announced during a local hospital steering team meeting, prior to activation. The SWAT Team leader quickly assembles a team of previously identified expert resources to rapidly and efficiently address workflow issues and to deal with any unintended consequences (see Chapter 9). SWAT Team meetings should be documented as part of activation communications so clinicians understand the decisions being made to resolve workflow-related issues.

SWAT Team members vary depending on the type and degree of changes being implemented. For example, if you were implementing CPOE, you would want physician and clinical leadership on the SWAT Team, as well as pharmacy representation. Workflow issues cannot be resolved in silos, and it is necessary to have everyone who is impacted by the process change involved in timely issue resolution.

When a physician enters an order in the system, for example, the order impacts both nursing and pharmacy workflow. A group of physicians trying to resolve a CPOE-related issue might derive a solution that works well for them, but which could negatively impact nursing and pharmacy workflows. Therefore, it's important to have the right people working to resolve these issues.

Technical Break-Fix Support Team
A technical support team on site enables the facility to have resources available on a timely basis for technical issues.

During Stage 1 of activation support, technical resources are assigned to the facility and are physically located on site to rapidly deal with any issues. The Stage 1 support team continues until at least a three-day period passes without any critical technical issues after activation. During Stage 2 support, the technical resources largely remain at their home base, but do work in shifts at the facility and are available after hours. During Stage 3 of activation support, technical support is available during normal business hours and is on-call during off hours.

Clinical Support
During activation, clinical at-the-elbow support ensures that resources are available to clinicians in their daily operations as they gain familiarity with the new system. Clinical support resources, including both project resources and facility super users, are assigned to each unit or department impacted by the transformation during Stage 1 to readily provide support wherever and whenever it is required.

During Stage 2 of activation, clinical support remains intact but the project support is no longer physically assigned to the unit. Station them instead in the command center and have them round regularly. This way, the clinicians begin to gain some independence in completing their work, but assistance is quickly and readily available if needed, as well as during rounding times. This is analogous to a toddler learning to walk; the clinicians are working somewhat independently but have support nearby in case they stumble. During Stage 3, clinical support staff are available in the command center to answer questions, and the number of support staff are reduced, while super users continue to provide at-the-elbow support at a facility.

It is critical to take the super users out of staffing, meaning that their primary role is to support clinicians, not provide patient care. This is especially vital during Stages 1 and 2, when the learning curve is steep. While there is a tendency to pull super users back into staffing during peak patient loads, you must continually emphasize how vital super users are to hardwiring the change and helping your staff gain comfort with the new tools. If a go-live is planned for a typically high census time, plan accordingly—meaning don't rely on your super users to fill the gaps. Beef up your staffing or borrow from another hospital or area within your organization to backfill so that the super users can do what they need to do to ensure success and strong adoption.

Other Support

Another form of support to offer comes in the form of *clinical transformation experts*. These are project team members with a full-time focus on clinical transformation activities. They are true workflow experts and, in many cases, participated in system design. They understand the intricasies of workflow processes and can round and help smooth out any workflow-related bumps—and then report these to the command center for communication to the masses, so that the processes become hardwired into action.

In addition, *application specialists* are EHR project team members who focus full-time on system design and installation activities. They have deep back-end system knowledge of how particular functionality works. Often these are the resources that did the build for the system. While they might not have strong clinical expertise, they do possess a solid understanding of system functionality and, coupled with a workflow expert, they can resolve issues as they arise.

THREE-TIER SUPPORT MODEL

Create a three-tier at-the-elbow support model for activations based on the previous descriptions:

- Tier 1: local super users and rolling super users.
- Tier 2: clinical transformation experts.
- Tier 3: EHR application specialists.

Implementation support is key to success and includes classroom instruction, as well as support staffing to help clinicians become proficient. Creative variations in physician training, including web-based training, video demonstrations, and CME-aligned programs, help busy clinicians learn how to use the system effectively. Then during go-lives, facilities provide at-the-elbow support for physicians and clinicians and help them cope with predictable, short-term productivity declines that occur during the transition.

How Much Support Is Enough and For How Long?

There is no magic number and, as described earlier, it really depends on how well your clinicians are trained, how engaged your super users are, how much change you are implementing, and the amount of functionality that is introduced. You will also find if you are a multi-facility health system, the first one or two activations will require more support and resources than later activations. This is because you will learn as you go. As a result of this learning, you will not only have fewer issues but more experience in dealing with them.

An example of activation support for CPOE go-lives is depicted in Table 7-1. As you can see, it really varies by organization and is dependent upon the factors previously mentioned.

Everybody Knows Their Roles

A transformation management initiative of this magnitude requires broad-based support and shared responsibilities, systemwide. Provide an activation toolkit ahead of time to everyone involved in the activation. The toolkit should explain how the command center at their facility will operate. The command center managers, as well as all other role players, should receive checklists in advance that delineate what their staff needs to do three weeks ahead of time, two weeks ahead of time, and so forth. You can't let any aspects of the implementation coast.

THE IMPORTANCE OF SURVEYING

As described earlier in this chapter, sometimes when making the rounds, leadership might encounter an anxious clinician or two and then conclude that all is not well. However, when they see the data that tell them that, let's say, fifty of the clinicians feel comfortable using the system on their own, it is reassuring.

Organization	# of Days of CPOE Support
Hospital A	5 days; leave 2 to 3 trainers onsite for 30 days
Hospital B	14 days; physician support on call for 30 days
Hospital C	14 days; physician analyst on call for 6 weeks after each go-live
Hospital D	14 days; 1 to 2 trainers onsite for 30 days
Hospital E	14 days; in house physician support on call for 30 days
Hospital F	3 days; 1 clinical analyst for ongoing support

Table 7-1: Case Examples of CPOE Support Requirements

The data concerning quality and regulatory compliance during an activation merits attention. You want to ensure that both in the short- and long-term, the data you need for the Department of Health and Human Services' Centers for Medicare & Medicaid Services (CMS) and The Joint Commission is captured accurately and appropriately. As clinicians are learning to use new tools, sometimes they may forget to document this information, or they may document it in the wrong place in the EHR. It is critical to engage the local team, who typically is responsible for auditing and reporting this information to CMS, during the activation. They should report this information to the local hospital steering team as well as the local managers, and they should remind clinicians how to document the information accurately and appropriately. It's important to catch bad habits early, before they become hardwired and permanent.

HARDWIRING THE TRANSFORMATION: WHAT'S NEXT AFTER ACTIVATION?

If a healthcare organization pays a small fortune for software but doesn't commit the resources necessary to offer the proper level of training and handle the people side of organizational transformation management, the transformation will turn out to be a debacle.

Does your executive leadership team have a sufficiently long-term perspective to support a large-scale transformation management initiative? If the perspective is too short, you can't even be in the game. If your project perspective is long enough, often sufficient time is available to devise strategies for overcoming hurdles.

Ultimately, the patient comes first. All the plans and activities must first relate to that fact. It is not sufficient to be strong in a few aspects of change management and hope that other things will simply click into place.

If your top executive leader has bought into the whole system and is an advocate, then all the better. In the case where one of your facility executives proves to be resistant, you need to devise alternative strategies to manage the resistance. Create compensation incentives tied to a successful launch and completion of the various project phases. Consider changing the job descriptions of managers to focus on accountability for the EHR.

The message is this: Leave nothing to chance if you can help it. Have a system in place for everything. Have a plan and implement that plan. Coordinate your resources. Test, monitor, and follow up. Ask for feedback. Listen long and hard. Then, repeat. Assembling the local hospital steering team several months prior to activation, for example, offers the best chance of creating the impetus that the project will require.

At the local hospital steering team meetings, deliver compelling metrics. Show participants how comfortable physicians are, for example, using the system on a scale of one to five. Track system use over a two-week period and then show the leadership group that their clinicians are gaining proficiency and will be able to effectively work with the system.

Keep the hospital steering teams focused on what is necessary to hard-wire the transformation during activation. Review with them the list of all the ongoing support they have in place and the importance of continually engaging super users. Show them that you even have a celebration event scheduled. Demonstrate that a go-live event only occurs after myriad checks and simulations have successfully been completed.

The local hospital steering team examines all of the system resources from soup to nuts, including the processes, the technology, and the people two weeks before go-live, when the go, no-go decision is made. There are a number of report forms and charts that can help them do this. To view various forms and charts related to activation, visit www.cicadvisory.com.

A huge army of people is involved in a facility's activation. It may seem that you have withdrawn, but actually you haven't. Dispense your resources judiciously and still heavily involve the team in monitoring.

MAINTAIN AND IMPROVE

One strategy to employ to hardwire the changes or, based on the transformation model, to "maintain and improve," is to devise a *transformation action plan*. This plan contains best practice recommendations for ensuring that old habits don't resurface and that the change remains intact. It contains step-by-step activities to complete on a monthly basis by role. After a month, two months, six months, and so on, clinicians remain in the loop, not merely as a result of their daily interaction with the EHR, but through a series of exercises, new aspects of the system to master, and other activities in which they are engaged. Remember, the third element in the transformation model, according to the methodology in Kotter's book *Our Iceberg Is Melting: Changing and Succeeding Under Any Conditions*, involves two major steps: "don't let up" and "create a new culture."[3]

After your initial success, press on harder and faster. Where applicable, leverage your momentum and credibility gained from short-term wins. Learn what's working, refine your plans, and then tackle even bigger aspects of the transformation. Align and monitor key organizational areas as needed or apparent, and sustain leadership involvement. Don't let up on ensuring that the new workflows and operations permeate all necessary levels in the hospital, and constantly ask for feedback.

In creating the new culture, applaud, nurture, and hold on to the new ways of behaving until they solidify and replace old traditions. Keep emphasizing how the changes are working and why the old ways are no longer applicable. Measure your progress department by department, and help to bolster the sustained performance.

Activation is only the beginning of the journey, not the end. Continue to monitor the emotional impact of the transition on the various teams throughout your facility. Transformation, quite simply, takes time.

Above all, ensure that your executive leadership continues to support and model the new behaviors for which the transformation management initiative was designed in the first place: to improve the quality of care in your organization.

INSIGHTS AND LESSONS LEARNED

- Large-scale transformation management initiatives require broad-based support and shared responsibilities systemwide, with everybody fully understanding their roles.
- Executive leadership at your facility must understand how much time it takes for a massive transformation initiative to work; if not, you can't be in the game.
- Leave little to chance, have a system in place for everything, implement your plan, coordinate your resources, test, monitor, follow up, seek feedback, listen well, and repeat.
- Applaud and nurture the new ways of behaving until they solidify and replace old traditions, measure your progress department by department, and help bolster the sustained performance.
- Ensure that your executive leadership continues to support and model the new behaviors that have been designed to put patients first, every day.

THINKING FORWARD

1. Have you identified your local hospital steering team(s)?
2. Do you have enough at-the-elbow support for clinicians at go-live?
3. How will you ensure that the transformation is hardwired?

REFERENCES

1.   Gawande A. The Checklist. *The Checklist Manifesto. How To Get Things Right.* New York: Metropolitan Books; 2009:35-47.

2.   Gladwell M. *The Tipping Point.* New York: Bay Back Books, 2002.

3.   Holger R, Kotter J. *Our Iceberg Is Melting: Changing and Succeeding Under Any Conditions.* New York: St. Martin's Press, 2005.

CHAPTER 8

Measurement and Reporting

INTRODUCTION

Unless you choose a destination for your journey, you don't know where you're going to end up. With so many healthcare institutions facing wide-ranging challenges in the implementation of EHRs, defining performance measures and tracking measurable benefits are fundamental for validating successful adoption.

Through your experience as transformation leaders, you will learn that technology tools will be adopted if their value and benefits can be effectively demonstrated and measured.

With any large-scale transformation project, the board of directors, as well as key stakeholders and the community at large, will want to know their return for investing time, energy, and financial resources. As a result, even your initial negotiations and contract with the software vendor should include mandatory performance measures tied to improvements in clinical outcomes.

Idenitify key clinical areas of focus that you want to improve. One example might be a reduction in patient falls, in emboli/deep vein thrombosis rates, or in time to treatment for acute myocardial infarction. Add these specific measurements to your vendor contract. This ensures that, from the outset, your software vendor is on the hook as much as you are.

CHARTING YOUR SUCCESS

Be ambitious as you establish your implementation methodology. Early on, make decisions about what type of performance measures will indicate success. For example, you might want to know how long it took a clinician to access the EHR. In the paper world, incredibly, sometimes it takes several days to access the records.

Often, in the paper world, if a record is being processed for, say, a patient discharge, considerable time and effort is required to retrieve it. At times when patients need to be hastily readmitted because of an acute situation, being unable to quickly and easily retrieve their records poses a major problem.

In one facility, it took on average 39 hours to access a historical medical record. Through automation, this was reduced to less than 30 minutes. Accessing records 78 times faster than previously—99 percent faster—is nothing short of an incredible improvement in clinicians' access to vital information.

Access to a patient's EHR, however, is only one of the many performance measures that can be identified, defined, and monitored. Because of such metrics, you will have the ability to determine whether or not you're doing what you said you would do.

Chapter 3 discussed the decision framework process that takes place early in the EHR implementation. With the maturation of your performance measurement program, hold a second decision day during which you invite executives from across the health system to evaluate and approve key performance measures. This promotes system-level adoption and buy-in. Ask each executive leader to "own" one of the performance measures and monitor it, as well as to resolve issues and remove barriers. In preparation for this event, it is important to do some diligent planning by conducting a thorough literature review to identify best practices and relevant performance measures based on the applications being implemented. In addition, poll other health systems to see what measurements they have in place. Ask them how the system benefits them, their physicians, clinicians, and most importantly, their patients.

PERFORMANCE MEASURES THAT COUNT

Collect a list of potential performance measures and present them to your senior leaders. They should reach consensus on key measures that you can employ and then monitor on an ongoing basis. Scaling down the list to a manageable number requires far less time than assembling the initial measures. Still, much analysis and debate may take place as to which are the most meaningful for your health system.

As you finalize the list, identify clinical champions for each measure. These champions become responsible for "approving" the benchmarks for comparison, data collection, and reporting to ensure ongoing optimization and reporting to senior management.

Beyond using measurement for overall systemwide implementation, employ pre- and post-activation–specific measures to determine the effectiveness of the transformation process. Several months before initiating an activation, develop standard definitions for baseline meaures in conjunction with the local leadership of a facility. These measures are used by your oversight committee to monitor adoption of the new tools and processes for each activation. However, for long-term optimization of data and reporting, it's important to focus on automation of the reporting processes so local owners can monitor and trend the data. This enables real-time reporting to executives and stakeholders who can use the information for ongoing improved decision making.

For example, if you are seeking to know how many people entered the ED but left without treatment, you would first work with your leadership team to establish a baseline number and the corresponding percentage. Such knowledge helps set the stage for productivity impact discussions with hospital leadership. When new processes are implemented, productivity declines significantly for a period of time, so it's important to measure the benefits. Clinicians will accept some temporary productivity declines if they can attain clear and legible clinical information 99 percent faster, and if such information helps them provide higher quality care.

During go-live, begin monitoring the measures chosen and sharing the results with your local leadership team in a blatantly transparent process. For the first two to four weeks in the activation period, depending on the amount of new workflows and processes being implemented, you should disseminate the results of these activation metrics daily to the facilities and various other departments. Gradually, you can reduce your rate of dissemination as the transformations become hardwired into daily practice.

CASE STUDY:
DEVELOPING A METHODOLOGY
TO EVALUATE SYSTEM CHANGES

By Patricia P. Sengstack, DNP, RN-BC, CPHIMS,
Deputy CIO and Chief, Clinical Informatics, NIH Clinical Center

In August 2004, the National Institutes of Health (NIH) Clinical Center (CC) in Bethesda, Maryland, implemented a new EHR. It replaced the legacy system that had been in use for nearly 30 years in the 240-bed federally-funded, biomedical research hospital, which accommodates nearly 10,000 new patients a year, with 95,000 outpatient visits a year. Included in the implementation was computerized provider order entry (CPOE) with order sets, clinical documentation, result retrieval from laboratory and radiology, and an integrated pharmacy system. The change was significant not only in terms of technical operations and maintenance, but from the clinician's perspective as well. The way users navigated through the various screens and accessed needed information for patient care was unfamiliar. It took months to fully appreciate the flexibility and potential of such a system. Over time though, clinicians realized many opportunities to enhance the system and potentially help streamline ineffective processes. The requests for changes and improvements began streaming in. It seemed as if every department and every institute at the NIH wanted a new electronic note or new process to support patient care and research. They wanted new modules added so the system could become their "one-stop shop." They wanted functionality to ensure patient safety, including methods to help limit the number of errors made while ordering and entering data. They wanted notification when results returned. They wanted images from other systems imbedded to improve workflow. They wanted new functionality that contained the latest bells and whistles the vendor offered. The deluge of requests left little time between various projects to evaluate their success.

Over the next few years, the list of projects and system changes continued to grow. A team from the IT department met for a strategic planning session and determined that system changes needed a methodology to be evaluated. Change after change was being inserted into the system, yet limited resources were allocated to answer questions such as: Was it successful? Was the business need met? Did the new pharmacy system reduce medication errors? Did adding relevant lab data to order forms reduce the incidence of overdosing? Did the alert that was created to stop nurses from inadvertently entering inaccurate heights and weights work? Did the creation of a new consolidated flowsheet reduce documentation time for nurses? Did the new patient portal result in increased patient satisfaction? Did the new one-page screen for patient medications improve accuracy of medication reconciliation? Did allowing the use of the "copy forward" feature in the system have an effect on the quality of physician progress notes? The importance of evaluating the effectiveness of various system implementations began to move up a level in terms of organizational priority as financial and resource requirements increased.

In fall 2008, the Outcomes Evaluation Group (OEG) was formed and asked to develop standard, repeatable methodologies to evaluate any project or initiative that was felt to be of high importance. This newly formed group included three members of the IT department, each with a clinical background. One team member was a nursing informatics specialist hired in a half-time position, strictly to work on the outcomes initiative. The other two members already had departmental responsibilities but were able to carve out approximately six to eight hours per week for outcomes work. One was a former respiratory therapist and the other a nursing informatics specialist who also served as the Deputy CIO. It is estimated that in total, .8 FTEs were devoted to IT evaluation.

Initial work of this group included an investigation of best practices for developing a health IT outcomes program. A literature review resulted in limited success in finding helpful documentation that provided guidelines or case studies in setting up a quality program to evaluate system implementations and enhancements. There were, however, two tools discovered that have provided a framework for carrying out outcomes projects that have been useful and have laid the foundation for the work of this group. These tools are:

1. **The Agency for Healthcare Research and Quality's (AHRQ) Health Information Technology Evaluation Toolkit.**[1] This toolkit provides step-by-step help through the process of planning an evaluation. It includes steps such as determining the goals for the evaluation, identifying metrics, and considerations for sample size. Also included are the various categories of evaluative studies that can be conducted (clinical outcomes measures, clinical process measures, provider adoption and attitude measures, patient adoption and attitude measures, workflow impact measures, and financial impact measures).

2. **The Statement on Reporting of Evaluation Studies in Health Informatics**[2] **(STARE – HI).** This publication provides clear and detailed descriptions on how an informatics evaluation should be documented, including how to write up each section of an evaluation publication (i.e., abstract, introduction, methods, results, discussion, and conclusion).

With the help of these resources, the team began with multiple brainstorming sessions and a large dry erase board. The AHRQ evaluation categories were written up on the board along with an additional category of Research Outcomes Measures, as NIH's focus is research. With these categories visually displayed, the OEG documented potential ideas for evaluation. The list of ideas was long. Obtaining input regarding prioritization was the next step in determining where to start. Several meetings with key organizational stakeholders from a variety of disciplines and departments led us to begin with a handful of projects on which to focus. We wanted to be realistic in terms of the complexity and size of the evaluation projects and, as a result, began our mission with the following initiatives:

- Evaluation of the accuracy of Intake & Output: pre-implementation of electronic ICU clinical documentation.
- Adoption and satisfaction of a new medication screen.
- Incidence and analysis of text copied forward in physician documentation.

- Effectiveness of an alert to stop entry of inaccurate heights and weights.

As with any research project, the details proved to be more difficult than initially thought. Deciding to evaluate effectiveness was only the first step. It took many hours or sometimes even days to determine exactly what to measure. Starting with a clear understanding of the reason for the implementation or system enhancement was essential. This provided the framework to establish metrics that would indicate whether or not the goal was met. The OEG has found this particular step in the evaluation process to be most challenging. For example, one evaluation effort was to look at the quality of physician progress notes since the electronic "copy forward" feature was activated in the system. The team struggled with the definition of quality. Considerable time was spent trying to answer the questions: What specific part of the physician progress note should be reviewed? What criteria will be used to determine high versus low quality? Who will make that determination? In fact, the answers to some of these questions were so elusive that the best metric at the initial phase of evaluation was simply to assess the incidence of copying forward physician assessments and plans (both free text fields). The team evaluated how often the assessment and plan sections were copied and then analyzed closely what appeared to be outliers or notes copied multiple times by different authors.

Another example is the evaluation project surrounding the effectiveness of an alert that was created to display when a nurse attempted to enter a height or weight that was 10 percent different than the previous weight. Challenges included the finding that sometimes the previous weight may have been the one that was wrong, and long periods of time may have elapsed between weights in the outpatient setting. Each evaluation conducted was unique in terms of what was measured. The lesson learned was that for top-priority projects, this discussion of measuring effectiveness needed to occur during the planning phase of implementation with the business owners or key stakeholders.

With a few projects underway or completed, the OEG team moved to a more proactive approach in determining opportunities for meaningful evaluation. In conjunction with the NIH Clinical Center's Project Management Office, a new process was added to the planning phase of all IT projects. This process included an assessment of whether or not a new project or initiative under consideration would warrant a formal evaluation to assess outcomes. If deemed a top priority, then during the planning phase, the discussion of metrics occurred. What should be measured? When should it be measured? Do we need to collect baseline data prior to project implementation? Who will collect the data? And once we have the data, what are we going to do with them? It was found to be important to have these types of discussions surrounding the data to make sure that the correct data were collected at the outset. The OEG discussed study design prior to any evaluation to help avoid this potential pitfall.

With any completed evaluation, the STARE-HI guidelines were used to document the study. Using these guidelines for each section of the write-up helped not only in preparing a quality deliverable, but also helped in the planning phase. Knowing and understanding the various areas to address in each section of the document assisted in ensuring that steps in the evaluation process were not missed as the project progressed. The OEG's goal is to publish the findings of at least one evaluation study annually. See Table 8-1 for a brief explanation of each of the four evaluative studies mentioned, along with their outcomes. The team continues to work toward improving its evaluation process, while at the same time providing valuable information that has the potential to improve the care and safety of the research patients at the NIH Clinical Center.

An Evaluation of the Accuracy of Intake & Output Calculations: Pre-implementation of Electronic ICU Clinical Documentation

- Evaluation Question: Does the current paper ICU flowsheet provide accurate calculations of intake and output?
- Random selection of 30 ICU patients
- Paper flowsheets reviewed and electronically re-calculated
- Discrepancies in calculations 63% of the time

Adoption and Satisfaction of a New Medication Screen – One Page View of All Patient Medications

- Evaluation Question: Do clinical staff find the new tool useful?
- N=54 (10%)
- 75% of users found the new "meds view" tab useful
- 67% reported that they would use it in their clinical practice and would recommend it to others
- Comments section extremely useful in making meaningful enhancements to the view

Incidence and Analysis of Text Copied Forward in Physician Documentation

- Conducted an evaluation of the use of the "copy forward" functionality in electronic clinical documentation
- Evaluation Question: How frequently is the "copy forward" functionality in the electronic health record being utilized by physicians in their progress notes?
- The Assessment section was evaluated retrospectively for a 2 1/2 year period from May 2007 - December 2009. (representing 55,000 progress notes)
- Assessment duplicated 14,159 times (26%)
- Duplication from notes authored by another physician = 7,085
- Majority of notes duplicated only once or twice with a range of 1–92 times
- Future analysis – evaluate actual and potential clinical impact of multi-instance copying

Effectiveness of an Alert to Stop Entry of Inaccurate Heights and Weights[3]

- Evaluation of the effectiveness of an alert for a weight entered that is 10% < or > the previous entry
- Evaluation Question: Did the alert stop inaccurate entry of weights?
- Looked at nurses' behavior in the electronic system after alert fired
- Alerts occurred in 2.74%, Nurses overrode 30.3% of True-Positive (TP) and 97.3% of False-Positive (FP) alerts.
- The alert has an acceptable FP rate and does not appear to cause nurses to change entries to satisfy the alert. The alert improves recording of patient weights.
- Future enhancement to the alert include:
  - Analysis of why TPs are being overridden
  - Length of time between weight entries
  - Patient's age

Table 8-1: Summary of Evaluative Studies

MEASUREMENT SPONSORSHIP

Even during the design of a phase, it's important to have people thinking about the measures that will be employed for performance measurement during and after activation. Early on, ask your leadership to consider the desired outcomes of implementing the new system and how best to demonstrate the benefits. From the top executives down to the user level, people need to ponder how they are going to measure success. You should constantly challenge them on this point.

When end users pay attention to appropriate performance measurement tools, the entire organization takes on a higher level of accountability. This is where the entire nation's healthcare delivery system is headed: everyone in the industry will be on the hook. Public and private accountable care organizations (ACOs) and the CMS Meaningful Use initiative are two critically important programs impacting health systems and providers nationwide and are both highly focused on evaluating performance based on specific quality measures. In fact, CMS proposed to harmonize quality measures for ACOs with Meaningful Use requirements and criteria.[4] So we will all have federal and state governments and private insurance companies monitoring our progress and performance to an even greater extent than previously experienced.

Measurement and reporting helps build a culture of accountability that will prepare you for meeting the environment of national healthcare reform. Quality measure data will provide increased transparency and accountability to meet evolving needs for reporting and electronic submission of clinical quality measures based on health outcomes. In many ways, as the journey continues for all of your facilities, and the challenges increase, the metrics become more important to the organization and all stakeholders in patient care. It may be worth noting to plan for integration of the clinical and operational quality measures that will evaluate ACOs and the achievement of Meaningful Use in your organization's own measures.

For each measure employed, identify executive sponsorship as well as related expert clinical sponsorship. First, ask executives to volunteer to sponsor a specific measure. With a measure related to quality, for example, confirm with the chief quality officer, "Here's a key measure that you've agreed to monitor. We want you to own it. We're counting on you to provide us with the data on a regular basis."

Ideally, each of your measures should be sponsored by a leader who owns that area. For example, a financial metric might be sponsored by the chief financial officer. A clinical metric might be sponsored by a chief nursing officer or a chief medical officer.

MEASURES IN MOTION

Once your project management team is comfortable with the measures chosen, ensure they are broad enough in scope, yet sufficiently focused, so as to provide the organization with a penetrating and insightful look at how adoption of the new system and transformation of the culture is proceeding.

One example measurement might deal with the percentage of verbal orders co-signed within 48 hours. As you likely know, a requirement from The Joint Commission directs physicians to co-sign verbal orders within 48 hours after giving them. From this measurement, you could spot increases or decreases in compliance. You can work with the Health Information Management department to run a report from the system indicating which physicians are not in compliance. Provide this list to the hospital physician leadership and then dispatch your physician champions and super users to show the noncompliant physicians how to sign their verbal orders electronically.

At first, physician leaders and department managers who are asked to run these daily measures might be skeptical that the system will help them to improve their numbers. They may not believe that their productivity or effectiveness is going to rise. Perhaps they have preconceived notions that processes simply don't get better. They certainly have no idea that their effectiveness and *compliance numbers* are likely to improve.

As an example, one hospital employing this metric process initially had less than 40 percent compliance with verbal order co-signatures. Today, across the board, compliance rates average 97 percent. This is a massive improvement and a great benefit, for both the patients and the hospital as a whole.

Perceptual Measures

Another example of a measurement to employ is physicans' and clinicans' perceptions of standardized care. Do this in preparation for a future phase in which physicians might be heavily impacted. The objective is to convince clinicians that offering care in a standardized way is highly desirable and is occurring as a result of the transformation.

Before engaging this measure at one organziation, the project team hypothesized that the nurses would report the delivery of care was not particularly standardized, because different clinicians deliver care in different ways. In contrast, the team surmised that the physicians themselves would say, "Sure, we're all standardized." The initial hypothesis proved to be correct: At the outset, delivery of care was not standardized, but this changed over time as the transformation took hold.

ADOPTION OF MEASURES

Spread the word that adoption of measures is necessary to ensure that all departments and all facilities continue to move through the implementation process as planned and to help monitor adoption on an ongoing basis.

Some examples of metrics employed throughout a project may include:

- Percent utilization of physician order entry.
- Decrease in medication error rates.
- Reduction in the number of clinically reported cases of catheter-associated urinary tract infections (UTIs).
- Reduction in the rate of clinically reported and significant hospital falls
- Coding/medical record deficiencies
- Net Revenue Improvement (charge description master, standardization, charge entry/capture, clinical denials)
- Clinician satisfaction with access to information

Table 8-2, "Benefit Measures," indicates the metric in columns one and two, the executive champion in column three, and a review of progress for each metric by month in the remaining columns.

ONE FACILITY VERSUS ANOTHER

In large health systems, the opportunity exists to measure one facility against another. In such instances, competition is a beautiful thing. When you meet with the project team of one facility and walk them through each metric of another facility, they have little reason to dispute the cold, hard facts. In the area of delinquent medical records, for

	Indicator	Executive Champion	2010			
			Aug	**Sep**	**Oct**	**Nov**
	Service - Clinical Adoption and Clinician / Physician Satisfaction					
2	Standardized care is given in ED- nurses*	xx	3.01		2.75	3.84
3	Clinical (non-physician) team satisfaction with access to information*	xx	2.75		3.09	3.42
	Outcomes - Safety and Quality					
6	% utilization of EMR documentation (PowerNote) by ED physicians	xx	96.8% ↑	95.2% ↓	95.9% ↑	91.8% ↓
7	% ED CPOE	xx	85.1% ↑	89.2% ↑	91.3% ↑	93.4% ↑
8	Decrease in medication error rates in ED	xx	0.24 ↓	0.38 ↑	0.27 ↓	0.21 ↓
10	Reduction in # of clinically reported cases of urinary catheter associated UTIs	xx	2.07 ↑	3.89 ↑	2.25 ↓	3.21 ↑
11	Reduction in rate of clinically reported significant hospital falls	xx	0.08 ↑	0.08 ↑	- ↓	0.10 ↑
13	Utilization of bar-coded patient identification bands in medication administration at point of use	xx	88.8% ↑	86.4% ↓	89.7% ↑	89.3% ↓
14	Inpatient verbal orders co-signed within 48 hours	xx	93.7% ↑	91.4% ↓	93.6% ↑	92.7% ↓

* Likert scale 1-5

Note 1: All performance measure ratings are hypothetical and do not represent actual results for any hospital or health system

Note 2: Arrows indicate increase or decrease in performance rating from prior month

Note 3: Executive champions set measurement targets

Table 8-2: Benefit Measures

example, one facility in an organization had low compliance. Another facility, however, was doing an excellent job by holding their physicians accountable. The facility doing poorly felt that holding their physicians to a higher level of accountability would be problematic.

When the project team began publishing the numbers and distributing them to the executive leaders at each facility, those with low compliance wondered why they couldn't operate the same way as everyone else. Sometimes the data are so revealing and improvements in other facilities are happening so fast that you rock their world. Transparency and judicious peer pressure can be quite motivating. Within the confines of a healthcare system, when everyone's performance is seen by all, no one wants to be in last place on *any* measure.

Most of the statistics are automatically generated by the system with little opportunity to fudge the numbers. If a facility is consistently behind on certain metrics, they need to focus their attention accordingly. Since every facility is measured by the same metrics, most excuses for poor performance quickly fall by the wayside.

ADDING A MEASURE

It's gratifying to create a culture in which physicians and clinicians are accountable for their performance. You will find along the way, however, that sometimes clinicians or hospital leadership want to measure the same things in different ways. In such instances, employ the same decision-making process as you do for other requests. The request should be handled by your governance groups. Invite the requester to present the case to the governing committee and to convince them why something should be done differently. This process assures standardization and keeps the list of measures manageable.

The process for approval of new measures, while rigorous, is clear to all. By making its way up the chain, every suggestion receives full consideration. You don't want to add any measures unless they significantly contribute to your overall effectiveness. Concurrently, remain alert to suggestions that merit strong consideration and perhaps final approval.

SUCCESS BREEDS ENTHUSIASM

As you provide feedback to departments within the hospital on their performance, a level of enthusiasm develops for the EHR. The positive feedback people receive as a result of their performance helps foster their complete buy-in and acceptance of the transformation. After all, who would want to abandon the EHR after experiencing such improvement? Who would want to impede progress when they see, day after day, that their scores are improving? Who could remain resistant after this? The faster and more ably you can provide people with feedback that affirms the direction you want them to take, the greater the chance that they'll stay on course.

Like the people who step on a bathroom scale every morning and chart their progress in the quest to lose weight, seeing improvements in the measures related to their own departments spurs employees to do even better. Soon, with this moving frame of reference, it's hard for people to remember how things used to be. A new, higher standard takes hold and becomes the norm. Think back to the time before computers populated everyone's desks and people carried mobile devices. How did we ever get work done? We did, but it's difficult to recall the nature of our activities back then.

People's frames of reference can change quickly. Suppose your foot bothered you for months on end. Then you had a medical procedure, and suddenly your foot was restored to normal. You're walking around and having fun. About a month after that, it's difficult to recall how you made do during the time you were immobile. Fortunately, sensations such as pain and discomfort can become distant memories. So, too, can an inefficient work process.

An emotional component frequently accompanies organizational transformations. You might run into an angry physician or an upset nurse around the halls, but that represents an anomaly. One angry person does not make a majority. You can show complainers that the rest of the team, and indeed, the entire department, is doing fine. "Squeaky wheels" do not stick out like they used to and no longer merit a disproportionate share of attention.

SCHOOLING THE CUSTOMER

Many elements of a transformation are painful. With so many of your organizational staff unaware of what bad implementations look like, you have to continually school them. The Danish movie *Babette's Feast* serves as a perfect analogy. Babette spends her small inheritance cooking a spectacular dinner for some of the villagers. Only one person at the table understands the quality and uniqueness of the meal and is raving the entire time. For the rest of the guests, it's simply dinner.

Send some of your super users to help support a go-live at another health system. Many of them may have never worked outside of your organization. If you follow the plan we have outlined, they will come back to you raving about how wonderful your own implementation has been and how fortunate you were to have such high levels of adoption success. Ask them to tell this story to your governance groups, versus the project team communicating this, and add their story to your communications, using their exact words. If you don't know what you've got, then you're not likely to be bowled over when you should be. Thus, it's important to keep key role players and stakeholders informed as to what they're receiving and, equally importantly, what they are able to avoid as a result of the system's implementation.

Creating more transparency within the organization, ensuring that everyone knows what's coming and signs off, and constantly offering your narrative garners respect, both for you as project manager and for the project management team as a whole.

Subtle Reminders

Consider the example of a consultant who always includes several items on his consulting invoices for which no charge is levied. Beyond charging for his services rendered and any material fees, the consultant might list extra items that were accomplished or offered and then next to such items a charge of $0.

The consultant purposely includes several invoice items for which there is no charge as a way of demonstrating to the client the full measure of the services provided and what was involved in their delivery. This technique helps keep clients attuned to the services they are receiving. Otherwise, it's easy for clients to have no knowledge of all the benefits they have received, to be aware of them and forget, or to know about them but not value them.

You might feel as if offering a constant narrative is not your responsibility to the people in your organization. However, if you don't give them one, they'll make up a story, and what they concoct on their own is often wrong. It's much better to make your narrative their reality.

The ongoing challenge is to keep explaining what you do, what the organization seeks to accomplish, and the benefits realized in the past, present, and projected for the future. In healthcare, a majority of staff have no experience and no frame of reference when dealing with a transformation of this magnitude. What's more, they have no one to turn to. For them, it's a brave new world. As a result, your job as a leader entails constant hand-holding.

Sometimes, executive leaders will think you're allocating your time ineffectively. When you are so focused on implementation, people might perceive that you are not committed to ongoing support. A fine balance is needed. You might have to explain to them that, say, 50 percent of your time is spent on maintenance, 40 percent on furthering your project, and the rest is the fleeting time you have to take on other challenges. At all times, keep them in the loop.

We've seen many healthcare transformation agents who are enthusiastic about the project and the implementation, but lose focus on the overall mission. Improving patient care is the driving force and it must go hand-in-hand with increasing efficiency. Maintaining these performance measures, and adding new measures as the project grows, has proven to be an effective method of communicating benefits realized over the life of the project and helps keep key staff and stakeholders engaged.

INSIGHTS AND LESSONS LEARNED

- To justify your large expenditure to all stakeholders, show them what they have received for the investment including mandatory improvements in clinical performance measures tied to your vendor contract.
- Contact providers similar to your own facility or organization to learn which measures of success they employ to determine their progress.
- Measuring departments or facilities against one another can prove beneficial; no one can dispute established facts, and your data might prompt rapid improvements among those groups who trail in performance.
- Offering a constant narrative is mandatory; otherwise, people concoct their own narrative, and it will be wrong. Make your perception their reality.
- You cannot escape the ongoing challenge of explaining what you do, what the organization seeks to accomplish, and what the benefits will be.

THINKING FORWARD

1. What are your metrics for your EHR implementation? How are they different for each implementation phase?
2. How can you use competition to improve performance?
3. Are any of your measures tied to meeting goals for Accountable Care and Meaningful Use?
4. Who are the champions (clinical and administrative) for each of your metrics?
5. Who are all the stakeholders that should be informed of your progress in this new age of transparency in performance reporting?
6. How can you use competition to improve your performance?
7. Can you automate the data collection and reporting of your metrics through your EHR? If not, what steps can be taken to make this happen?

REFERENCES

1. Cusack CM, Byrne CM, Hook JM, et al. Health information technology evaluation toolkit: 2009 update. Rockville, MD: Agency for Healthcare Research and Quality, AHRQ Publication No. 09-0083-EF.

2. Talman J, Ammenwerth E, Brender J, et al. STARE-HI—Statement on reporting of Evaluation Studies in Health Informatics. *Int J Med Inform* 2009; 78(1), 1-9.

3. Cimino J, Farnum L, Cochran K, et al. Interpreting nurses' responses to clinical documentation alerts. AMIA 2010 Symposium Proceedings, 116-120.

4. *Federal Register*. Vol. 76, No. 67. April 7, 2011. II(E)(2)(a)(2). Scoring Methodology. p. 19569.

CHAPTER 9

Project Management – Making it Work

INTRODUCTION

In preparation for the launch of an EHR, it is best to assemble a project management office, staffed by professional and formally trained project managers, to lead the transformation initiative. By having an office entirely dedicated to the project, you're equipped to stay on scope, stay on time, and maintain effective communication.

Those who haven't previously worked on large-scale projects do not realize that before the project begins, earlier activities actually put the project in motion. Establishing a long-term organizational transformation initiative requires its own budget, scope of work, and time line to arrive at the point where the implementation of the project actually begins. Hence, you need to establish a budget for the preliminary activities that will actually put the large, long-term project in motion. This is especially true when project management is new for you, if a project of great magnitude is new for your organization, or if the system you're implementing represents a major leap for you.

For smaller providers engaged in pre-planning for a significant implementation, the number of staff that you involve depends on the size and scope of your organization. For one hospital, you'll probably have only one person involved in pre-planning and work with a simple financial structure.

BEST GUESSTIMATES

At the outset, you might have no idea as to what the overall budget or time line ought to be. Do some networking to gauge this or consider getting some experienced outside assistance for this important planning. You'll have to sketch out in advance what it will cost to staff up, and then with your top executives, produce a budget for one total project costs and return on investment depending on whether you're planning for one year, three years, five years, or more.

Regardless of the size of your organization, resources need to be put aside for the preplanning process in order to attain a realistic grasp of the project scope, the available resources, and the project objectives.

Large, well-managed EHR implementations benefit greatly from up-front planning and budgeting that spans many years. As such, the project team doesn't need to appeal for funds every year, saying "We're going to need another $5 million." Take the time to adequately preplan. Top leaders need to map out in advance how much everything will cost, and then hand the team a roadmap. This is a key driver of success.

EARLY MISTAKES

At one hospital, staff had received project management training but had not implemented a large-scale project management methodology or EHR system implementation. The project team attempted to use local talent instead of more expensive consultants and believed that such experience could serve as a foundation for success. One of the key people employed had implemented radiology systems software in hospitals, and this person was expected to become adept at a much larger implementation, such as an EHR project.

There was a comprehensive project plan with many interconnecting parts, and the team felt that it was necessary to keep them linked since resources were being shared across projects and all parts of the plan were key to overall success. Once the radiology software expert was in place, he wanted to dismantle current plans, hoping to make things simpler. He was not ego-involved, seeking to make his mark or taking action merely to do something. His project methodology basically clashed with the team's and was not typically the type of methodology employed for large-scale complex projects. Thereafter, the team understood the need to work with those who have already participated in a large-scale EHR implementation based on transformational principles.

In this instance, the project team was committed to an integrated approach to transformation management in devising the system, initiating training programs, and maintaining effective communication. For success to take place in a project of this size and scope, all of the pieces and parts need to be linked together and managed under one program.

STICKING WITH THE BASICS

Focus on using fairly standard tools, establishing priorities, identifying risks, and managing issues in accordance with an online project management software program. Project management software enables you to track progress, highlight issues, compile status reports, and remain on target. If you represent a smaller facility and don't want to invest in project management software, there are simpler tools available. The choice is up to you as long as you have an effective tool to keep your project on track.

Conduct weekly project management reviews. Outline the pros and cons of various decisions that confront you, keeping in mind the financial implications. If you feel a need to change the scope of the project, examine the potential impact on milestones, resource requirements, and desired outcomes before seeking approval.

With software management tools that contain online dashboards, easy access is afforded to those who require it and the dashboards provide considerable transparency. Anyone on the project team, including your top executives and other executive staff with responsibility for the program, can go online, day or night, and examine your progress, review open issues, monitor progress toward milestones, or obtain timely status reports.

THE QUEST FOR CONTAINMENT

One of the fundamental lessons learned from the early days of project management, which becomes more important once you have gone into a high support mode of the EHR, is to *keep telling the story*. Document what resources you have employed and how, in going forward, those resources will support the activation as well as future phases and future implementations.

All along, keep reinforcing for clinicians what's in it for them, and as they're exposed to more aspects of the technology, build upon the relationships you have with them.

You will see their eyes light up when you implement new parts of the system. They'll say, "Oh, it can do that?" A very normal part of the process is recognizing that the demand for what you can do for clinicians exceeds your capacity to provide it. Thus, the need to be more disciplined in documenting your time and resources, as well as allowing your end-user clinicians to make the choices in how they prioritize system improvements, is extremely important.

Communicate to your growing base of enthusiastic clinicians about the ways in which you spend your time. Typically, about 50 to 60 percent of your time will be devoted to system maintenance alone. The time left over each month could be devoted to helping clinicians enhance what they already have.

Ask your clinicians, "What are the most important things you want us to work on?" What is important to them will continue to spark their enthusiasm and initiative in adopting and implementing the EHR. Follow up by creating and relying upon a multidisciplinary group that reviews and prioritizes a growing list of enhancements. It is very normal once you have implemented the EHR to have clinicians ask for more functionality and enhancements to the system, so you need to plan accordingly.

If you have a small team, don't bite off more than you can chew. After you and your clinicians have identified what is most important, have the strength to walk away from lesser functions and features. It would be nice to do it all, but reality dictates that you cannot.

You have to exercise your decision-making muscle and continue making hard and practical choices on a regular basis. It's easy to get caught up in a trap of becoming a slave to others' excitement—they see what the system can do and then they want even more benefits. You're so thrilled to have the positive feedback that you attempt to promise everything to everybody. Project management on this level can be challenging. While you might work far more than 2,000 hours a year, you can't work 3,000 or 4,000. You only have so much time and so much energy. Keep your team from burning out and stay ready for whatever comes next.

We all are enticed by unending possibilities in terms of technology. If you buy a smart phone, soon you encounter untold add-ons.

Thousands of new apps are available every month. If you buy an eBook reader, you can end up ordering books far beyond your ability to read them. Meanwhile, your bill skyrockets. It would be nice to justify the extra expenses you incur by the knowledge you're gaining from all that extra reading, but this is not realistic. The same is true for project management; you need to make choices and prioritize based on the needs of your organization.

Managing Expectations

How clinicians perceive what the system will do for them means everything to them. So, keep them informed, aligned, and realistic. While encouraging their enthusiasm, corral their expectations. Help them to stay focused on the prize, which is to improve the quality of care in your organization, markedly decrease medical errors, help people get better as a result of coming to your facility, and improve overall efficiency.

Beware of clinicians who become enamored with the bells and whistles. Stay attuned to whether or not their requests actually support the key clinical and business needs and workflows. Even then, you have to prioritize. You have to do what is realistic, and you have to ask your clinicians what are the most important things you can do for them. It is not practical to implement many of the requests and ideas that you receive. Do not get sidetracked and, above all, prioritize.

TRANSFORMATION MANAGEMENT VERSUS PROJECT MANAGEMENT

A project might, or might not, represent a significant paradigm shift for the organization, and many projects are designed merely to maintain an organization's systems, processes, or assets. Conversely, transformation management requires project management to reach desired goals. Briefly, the methodology we have described is a logical set of planned and intentional interventions designed to transition an organization between old and new business processes and from old and new systems. It focuses on responding to the human dynamics of change—the make or break factor in a transformation campaign.

Selecting a transformation management methodology, such as Kotter's eight-step methodology and the transformation model referenced and illustrated in Chapter 2, provides a continuing guidepost on the path to implementation. Effectively managing organizational transitions also includes strategies for reducing the emotional impact, as well as managing any resistance.

Any organization undergoing major transformation is replete with "backdrops" that set the stage for the strategy chosen. Hence, past reaction to paradigm-shifting initatives should be considered, stretching back five years, on a facility level and by department, as should any disruption that occurred within a facility or department.

Transformation management, with respect to an EHR, involves assisting executive leadership, physicians, and employees at every level to understand the overall objective and their respective roles in achieving it. Throughout an implementation, a project mission statement guides both the team and, ultimately, all employees involved in the effort.

Readiness for organizational transformation can be measured by performing a baseline survey. Identifying your key stakeholders and assessing their readiness helps determine how all role players will be impacted by the transformation. Monitoring tools for tracking the impact on role players include the pre- and post-readiness surveys, attendance at events, and training records.

Key Elements

Beyond adopting a transformation management methodology, other effective elements of instituting large-scale change programs include:
- Establishing a governance structure.
- Establishing key stakeholders.
- Identifying required tools, techniques, and milestones.
- Establishing roles and responsibilities.
- Preparing negation plans for risk and resistance.

Before engaging a facility's leadership for support in the overall initiative, you want to have a well-developed training model including such elements as:
- Training methodology approach.
- Clinician training requirements.
- Classroom prerequisites.
- Training materials and logistics.
- Training communications plan.

With these factors in place, you should then customize your transformation management engagement to the hospital, taking into consideration the culture and receptiveness to the new and future modes of operation.

CASE STUDY:
BEYOND SYSTEM SELECTION: IT PROJECT MANAGEMENT IN A RURAL HOSPITAL

By Jessie Diaz, MBA, CPHIMS, Vice President and Chief Information Officer, Phoebe Putney Health System and Robert Collins, President, NEOS Technologies

Transforming a rural hospital from paper to the electronic world of clinical documentation and computerized provider orders requires a more personal approach to project management. These hospitals face enormous financial, operational, and technological challenges. Access to capital is often limited, making it difficult to keep technology updated and adequately staff IT projects. Most rural hospitals also find it difficult to allow outsiders to review their everyday practices in any great detail. These organizational challenges often create an environment of uncertainty and resistance to change. In addition, facilities often do not have the skill sets required to undertake the challenge of implementing an electronic system.

Phoebe Putney Health System (PPHS) is a network of hospitals, family medicine clinics, rehab facilities, auxiliary services, and medical education training facilities in southwest Georgia. Patient safety initiatives, regulatory changes, and Meaningful Use were a few of the factors that drove the organization to undertake the implementation of an electronic system. The senior management team knew that effectively transitioning from paper documentation and orders to electronic would be a significant undertaking that would require not only the staff to change but the culture as well. Changing the culture of any organization is a long-term, time-consuming, and emotionally charged quest that requires strong leadership, patience, wisdom, and more patience. Implementing electronic clinical documentation would be difficult, but asking physicians to enter specific orders through a computer system instead of writing whatever they wished would be like climbing a very large, steep, rocky mountain.

As a rural health system, recruiting and retaining first-class physicians to enhance and implement new services is both a top priority and a challenge. To accomplish this goal, PPHS had to be creative and often allowed physicians to govern themselves with little or no pressure to enact change from the senior management team or the board of directors. This offered physicians something they could not find in larger urban hospitals. It meant, however, that obtaining the physician buy-in would be a critical step to the adoption of the new electronic record.

The *beginning of transformation* starts at the top with vision and purpose. The first priority of the transformation to the EHR was to engage key personnel and create a strategy. The vice president of nursing and CIO engaged the CMO in creating the Clinical Transformation Executive Committee. The new committee consisted of senior management, physician leadership, and a clinical system vendor representative. The goal of the group was to create a high-level, overall strategy for the transformation from paper to electronic. The areas the committee focused on were program identity, goals, governance, resources, and culture change.

The committee developed a philosophy to guide the transformation: people, processes, and applications encompassing all areas of the clinical continuum to enhance and improve patient safety, quality of care, and workflow centered on and around the patient. Decisions always kept the patient at the center of safety, quality, and workflow. Defining this philosophy was the first step in creating the identity and goals of the project.

The committee laid out the time lines and the order of applications to be implemented in a *roadmap*. The emergency center would be the first department to complete documentation and orders electronically, followed by the surgery department. A new medication administration application would be implemented to provide tighter integration to electronic documentation and then all inpatient areas would begin utilizing the electronic system for documentation. A new order entry application would be implemented for the inpatient areas to be initially used by nursing and clinical support departments. The order entry application would be the foundation for the computerized provider order entry (CPOE). Implementing CPOE would be the last application to be put into use.

The interdisciplinary Clinical Transformation Executive Committee's strategy was to enhance the existing physician portal by adding medication administrations and clinical documentation for physicians to review before placing orders. Lab and radiology results, as well as medications, could already be accessed through the portal. This phase of the roadmap included the basics for the EHR and was planned to take several years to complete due to the complexity of PPHS, the culture, and applications being implemented.

Governance is required to bring about collaboration, standardization, and agreement in an environment of individuals advocating with different degrees of passion for their patients, employees, and themselves. Two steering committees were created: Documentation and Orders and a Physician Advisory Group. Each steering committee would report to the Clinical Transformation Executive Committee. The Physician Advisory Group reported through the Clinical Transformation Executive Committee and the Medical Executive Committee. The Steering Committees' responsibilities included:

- **Scope Management:** Developing and managing the scope of the implementation and change within the organization.
- **Work Plan Management:** Developing and managing the detailed work plan, milestones, and resource commitments and communicating these to the project teams to achieve success.
- **Risk Management:** Identifying and developing risk mitigation plans and reporting/escalating any potential risks that might impede the success of the project.
- **Communication Management:** Developing and executing a communication plan to maintain awareness, executive sponsorship, and buy-in for transformation's success.

The committees also played a critical role in leading the organization through the transformation. Membership on the committee included leadership from nursing, radiology, laboratory, respiratory, patient safety, quality, financial services, information technology, and the application project team. The committee was chaired by a nurse and physician.

The Physician Advisory Group was charged with providing guidance to the organization on behalf of the physician population on application utilization, workflow, and adoption. Membership consisted of physicians from each of the medical/surgical departments.

Resources transform a thought, vision, or plan into reality. A team of clinical and information technology professionals was needed. The committee looked within PPHS to find someone with the appropriate skill set in management, clinical processes, and technology to manage and oversee the quest for transformation. Not finding anyone, the committee chose to hire outside consulting support to provide a project manager to assist PPHS through the process. The rest of the core project team members were chosen for their specific areas of expertise. The core team members consisted of an emergency center, a surgery department, and an inpatient nurse for working with nursing on workflow transformation and applications setup, a nurse for training, and a pharmacist for CPOE. The team also had access to technical team members for personal computer, server, and network support. The extended team consisted of super users throughout the organization. The super users were instrumental for understanding existing workflow, designing future workflow, training, providing support of the new workflows and applications, and most importantly, communicating in a positive way about the change. The project team spent much of its time focused on getting the application set up and tested. The super users led the charge in terms of implementation and this, ultimately, led to the success of the transformation.

Managing the implementation is overwhelming and required managing the scope and expectations of the project. One common expectation was that the application would not affect the way patients were cared for and, therefore, would not greatly affect individual clinicians. This attitude created a barrier to transformation. Communicating that the applications would not affect the physical interaction but would impact patient safety and the quality and timeliness of care was paramount to gaining understanding.

Methodology
A project charter was created to provide the baseline for managing the scope and expectations. An online project management information system was utilized to track, communicate, and document milestones, tasks, issues, and risks. Milestones were cre-

ated and approved by the steering committees. The project team worked from a defined set of tasks. Issues were tracked as barriers to completing the tasks were encountered. If the issue could not be resolved, it was moved to the risk category. The project management methodology followed the Project Management Institute standards.

Communication

The team used multiple avenues to communicate the philosophy, goals, status, and culture change throughout PPHS. The mechanisms included emails, newsletters, meetings, flyers, table tents, digital signage, training, and one-on-one encounters. The team also enlisted the help of marketing professionals to craft unified messages. The challenge was communicating the appropriate message at the right time.

Workflow

The project team undertook workflow analysis at the beginning of the project by holding work sessions with the different areas throughout PPHS. The work sessions consisted of gaining an understanding of the current workflow and communicating changes for the future. The information gained was utilized to set up the applications, training, and communication. The changes in workflow were communicated through the Clinical Transformation Executive Committee, steering committees, Physician Advisory Group, and various organizational committees for approval. The teams implemented any future workflow in advance of the go-live if the application was not required. For example, the CMIO, along with the Physician Advisory Committee, Quality, and the Evidence-Based Coordinator standardized order sets on paper prior to the implementation of CPOE. The ownership of the workflow changes resided with the leadership of each area of PPHS.

Testing

Once the setup of the application was complete, super users were trained and given access to the system in both a controlled and non-controlled environment. In the controlled environment, patient scenarios were executed to test the application. Project team members were available to super users to answer questions regarding the setup and discuss potential revisions based on testing. In a non-controlled environment, the super users would test the application in their departments and provide feedback to the project team.

Training

Training consisted of classroom lectures, demonstrations, and practice of functions and new workflow taught by super users. Functional training of the application was set up to follow the workflow process. Although workflow was discussed at training classes, it was the responsibility of the departments to implement and monitor. Practice sessions were mandated as a follow-up to training. Each person trained had to complete a minimum of two practice sessions. Super users provided a proctored environment for practice sessions. A competency test was completed during the practice sessions. Additional practice sessions were required for those not passing the competency test.

Activation

The applications were implemented at different times throughout the transformation. Documentation and orders were implemented house-wide at the same time for nursing. A command center was set up with super users providing close support for end users. Typically, there was one super user per area per shift for the first two weeks. The command center stayed available to end users for seven to fourteen days, depending on the application being implemented.

Transformation happens as an intention of change. The implementation was just the first step in the transformation process. Using the EHR successfully to improve efficiencies, communication, patient safety, and outcomes is the true test of transformation. True transformation did not happen immediately upon activation of the applications. It took time for the organization to adapt.

PPHS has been on the electronic system for approximately one year with more enhancements and applications underway. It has not been an easy quest for electronic transformation and it is far from complete, but the initial barriers have been surpassed.

Transformation should be looked at as a process requiring strong leadership for governance, clear expectations, and team members ready, willing, and able to undertake the quest.

MOST PROJECTS FAIL

It might not be widely known, but most projects fail. Data from the Project Management Institute and other sources indicate that one quarter of all large institution projects are abandoned without ever reaching a successful conclusion.[1] Of the projects that do get completed, as many as three out of four exceed the established budget or extend past the established timeframes.

Too many organizations, hospitals among them, approach project management with a cookie-cutter mentality. They believe that by plugging in new project management software, following established timeframes, and dispensing resources accordingly, project success will be in their grasp. The real challenge on projects, however, tends to be deploying and eliciting commitment from your organization's human resources.

Allen Evitts, the founder of Essential Project Manager, observes that while organizations strive for consistency and seek to have all aspects of all project phases be measurable and traceable, "variation in human capabilities as well as interactivity results in the need for each project and each project phase to be viewed separately."[2] He notes that the key factor of effective project management is communication, specifically interpersonal communication. Everyone involved in a project has a role to play in terms of effectively communicating with others, the project directors most of all.

Often, organizations get caught up in micro-directing or micro-managing a project. This happens when the project leader is predisposed to hanging on to too many seemingly critical tasks, instead of engaging the skills and capabilities of the project team. Project leaders who devote ultra-long hours micro-managing a project actually put it in jeopardy.

No one is omniscient. No one can be on top of everything all the time. What's worse, by not tapping into the capabilities and skills of the project team, the project leader is forsaking vital resources that could free up his or her time, as well as keep all phases of the project on a more even keel.

Project teams experience development stages. Personality conflicts within and among the project team will occur. Just as you prepare your hospital or each department for the coming transformation, continually prepare your own project team to work effectively with one another. Paying constant attention to project management tools such as tasks, graphs, and charts—with a keen focus on meeting all milestones—is admirable, but may be shortsighted. The project leader who maintains a technical approach to leadership, while not recognizing the importance of interpersonal communications, might be putting the entire project at risk.

Quality, not Quantity

Staying on course, promptly issuing assignments, and dispensing project resources judiciously, in and of themselves, are just a few aspects of effective project leadership. The quality of individual performances, in the end, is what counts. Each task performed by each project team member cumulatively adds up to superior organizational performance. In other words, it is the qualitative as well as the quantitative aspects of the milestones accomplished and resources expended that count.

Without maintaining that fine balance, the project can be headed off course without the project leader's awareness. Spending too much time focusing on data and not enough time out and about with the numerous individuals whose work and daily activities will spell project failure or success is a common faux pas among otherwise effective project leaders.

Unmistakably, it is important to keep projects on track. Appropriately dole out funds, secure needed equipment, and issue assignments effectively. Concurrently, it is important to remain focused on the big picture of the project mission and what the organization, as well as all the role players, seek to accomplish.

THE ATTRIBUTES OF THE
SUCCESSFUL PROJECT MANAGER

A project manager represents huge and vital organizational initiatives, and that person's reputation precedes him or her, particularly in meetings with hotly contested issues. When a project manager walks the halls, he or she will often be recognized. This individual symbolizes the face of the project for the organization. That has its benefits, as well as its drawbacks.

Because a project manager is a harbinger of transformation, some people do not welcome his or her arrival. It's hard for some to accept all of the changes that the project entails. After surmounting specific project hurdles, however, a project manager earns respect as well. People begin to think, "He knows what he's doing."

Successful project managers need to be able to apply both hard and soft project management skills. The hard skills are those taught by organizations such as the Project Management Institute, universities, and special executive programs. Hard skills involve understanding and being able to apply the basics of project management: developing a scope of work; establishing a project plan; choosing milestones and time lines; and accounting for equipment, labor, and other capital resources.

Hard skills require rigorous study, but in and of themselves do not equate to effective project management. Indeed, if hard skills were all that were required, most project managers would be successful the majority of the time, and the projects they managed would unfold as desired and according to plan. This is simply not the case.

The answer to effective project management must involve the soft skills. These skills include offering clear and appropriate assignments, providing feedback at critical junctures, listening effectively, conducting performance appraisals, and effectively working with the variety of project role players and stakeholders.

OTHER SOFT SKILLS

Added to those fundamental soft skills, a variety of other management skills invariably prove to be vital, especially on longer, multi-phased projects. These skills include the following:

Developing Decision-making Capabilities

Making effective decisions is crucial for project managers who want to be successful. In the start-up phase, and especially once a project is in full stride, a project manager will continually be confronted by decisions that need to be made quickly, sometimes in the absence of helpful data, and sometimes to the disappointment of others.

The project team and other role players and stakeholders are all counting on the decisions you make and the direction the project takes.

The more confident and effective you are in airing your decisions, the less uncertainty and second-guessing you will encounter on the part of those who are impacted by your decisions.

Independent of your level of experience, continually hone and refine your decision-making skills. Whether you take a course, read books or articles, or observe the techniques of others who are effective decision makers, it pays to invest in yourself. You're probably already decent at decision making, and it was likely one of the reasons why you were chosen to head up the project to begin with. Now, show them what you've got by getting even better in a skill area where you are already adept.

Being Open to New Ideas

The ideas, suggestions, and observations of your team members, as well as other project role players and stakeholders, can prove to be quite valuable. Whenever someone has a money or time-saving idea that results in greater productivity or profitability, why not lend an ear?

No one can be on top of everything all the time and have all the right answers. Your immediate project team members undoubtedly possess a range of experiences, talents, and skills that greatly exceed what any one person possesses. Encourage them to offer their observations and ideas. You always have the option of discarding them, as you deem appropriate. More often than you might presume, you'll be handed a gem of a suggestion that is worth putting into practice with full vigor.

Providing and Being Open to Constructive Criticism

Related to the previous discussion, everyone needs appropriate feedback, including you. Feedback lets people know about the effectiveness or ineffectiveness of their performance. Criticism is a subset of feedback focusing on individual performance that might require correction, or for which room for improvement is apparent.

Provide formal education to your team on this topic, and incorporate it into your daily operations. This helps to break down barriers and also helps with the forming, storming, and norming phases typically seen as teams come together. It teaches the team accountability in owning issues and resolving them through focused feedback.

Being able to offer constructive criticism is a fine and gentle art. If you're not sufficiently forceful, this form of feedback will not be effective. If you're overly forceful, the recipient might resent it. Project managers walk a fine line between providing effective constructive criticism and being overly critical and potentially upsetting the recipient. It's a huge feather in the cap of the project manager who is adept in this element of soft skills, and has a well-developed sense of how to both offer as well as receive constructive criticism.

Managing Your Time

Time management and self-management skills are vital in project management. The project manager who wastes time on low-priority issues ends up either working long hours or putting the project in jeopardy. Managing one's time well requires some personal organization, itself a form of self-management. This means having the discipline to put things in their proper place, to pay attention to schedules, and most importantly, to recognize that of all project resources, your time, and how you dispense it, are crucial.

Having a Sense of Humor

After all is said and done, you have to be able to periodically enjoy a good laugh, and encourage your staff to do so as well. Conducting a long-term transformation campaign in a hospital setting is no easy feat. Laughter, it has been shown, helps you to maintain a sense of equilibrium.

Surprises will happen. Roadblocks and setbacks will appear out of nowhere. Most can be quickly resolved. However, some represent sizable problems and end up consuming time, money, and resources. Thus, ensure that your laughter quotient is high. Look for the mirth in what otherwise could be a disconcerting situation. It'll help keep you sane, help keep your project team in balance, and offer you the best chance of maintaining a healthy perspective.

In addition to displaying a sense of humor, have other release mechanisms in place, such as taking time out, going for a stroll, or simply removing yourself from your desk or office so as to clear your head.

CASE STUDY:
DEVELOPING PROJECT MANAGEMENT
GUIDELINES AND TOOLS

By Kristen O'Shea, MS, RN, NEA-BC, Vice President of Patient Care Services, Gettysburg Hospital, Gettysburg, Pennsylvania, and Clinical Transformation Officer, WellSpan Health, York, Pennsylvania

In 2007, WellSpan Health, an integrated healthcare system in south central Pennsylvania, started the critical work to build its EHR. Prior to that time, there were bits and pieces of an electronic record: laboratory results, orders management, and even an electronic form for the documentation of the nursing admission assessment. The work, initiated in 2007, however, was different; it was based on a solid project management framework and was designed to lay the foundation for most of the informatics work that would follow.

The project team had learned many lessons from its previous work to implement the nursing admission assessment. In that implementation, well-intentioned individuals worked to build a form to replicate the existing admission assessment. The group created data elements to reflect current practices across two very different hospitals. The result was an admission form that highlighted the disparities between the two hospitals. In the months following the implementation, there were many lessons learned as nursing leadership at the two organizations tried to understand what was happening with the new form. All of these lessons have evolved into critical success factors for WellSpan's clinical transformation efforts.

Project management is an essential component of a successful transformation project. WellSpan had not previously used a project manager with the admission assessment project and the results reflected this decision. It took a long time, design decisions were not documented, and needed resources were not obtained. Therefore, in 2007, before embarking on the design and build of all of the remaining nursing documentation and the electronic medication administration record (eMAR), a project manager was assigned. The project manager utilized a methodology that included tools and documentation that helped us to assure that this project would go as planned.

As the project began, a charter was drafted and clear roles and responsibilities were defined. The scope was crafted so that everyone from the IT team to the end users knew what to expect. As the executive sponsor, I learned that involvement and engagement were critical. Involvement is different from supportive enthusiasm. Involvement means knowing the status of the work and understanding fully when there are issues that need to be vetted at a level different from the project team. This had been a huge issue in our admission assessment project. Nursing leaders learned of the controversial issues and decisions after the form was in production. The project team had no clear place to take issues; so in many cases, they made decisions that would later cause us concern. For example, they created wording within the admission form itself that allowed for differences between the two hospitals. In some cases, these differences were logical and understandable; however, in other cases, they were unintended and a result of conflict without a clear mechanism for reaching decisions.

In order to avoid such problems from happening again, a leadership structure was designed that would allow for these types of decisions to be vetted. Every Monday morning, the project team leaders, including the project manager, the nursing informatics team, and the clinical analyst team leaders, would meet with nursing leadership from both hospitals to discuss design decisions in which there was conflict between parties. In addition, this team determined how to support and leverage clinical involvement at every step in the process, from assuring staff participation in design, testing, education, and having super users at the elbows of their peers during go-live.

Clinical leadership is a critical factor in the success of this type of work. As the team embraces that this is not another IT project, but one that clearly has clinical benefit and impact, its engagement grows. The team fully supported an "all hands on deck" philosophy with the go-live of the nursing documentation, so that clinical leaders not only knew how to use the system, but also could assist in triaging issues by knowing the top ten troubleshooting tips. Our staff knew that they were supported during the go-live. Clinician super users were scheduled 24/7 on clinical units and were well-versed in use of the system because they had been teaching its use during the weeks prior to go-live. WellSpan leverages about 10 percent of staff to be super users; however, we were thankfully also able to utilize exempt staff such as clinical nurse specialists and clinical educators to augment the pool of super users for those areas where 10 percent was not possible.

The design work was based on guiding principles that were agreed upon by the project team, as well as the leadership. These guiding principles also served as a gauge to determine if future attention or discussion was needed on the leadership side. For instance, if the group determined that the process might be different at the two hospitals, it violated one of the guiding principles and would be placed on the agenda for the Nursing Leadership/IT Monday morning meeting. The guiding principles created by the team were:

Safety First
- Minimize error.
- Build/use alerts.

Process-driven Design
- It's not just about computer forms.
- Clinical process is defined.
- It's important to communicate—not simply document.

Efficiency
- Minimize re-work and workarounds.
- If there are any, identify up front that they are temporary.

It Needs to Be Intuitive
- You don't need a paper explanation to do it.

Minimize Variations Across the System—Focus On:
- Best practice.
- Evidence-based practice.
- Standards.

Evaluate/Communicate Logical Differences
- Small community versus teaching hospital.
- Rehab versus acute care.

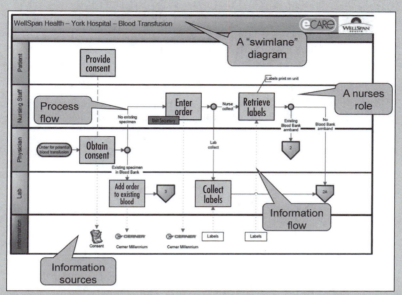

Figure 9-1: Swim Lanes

Avoid Redundancy

There were a number of tools that were employed that supported the guiding principles. Three tools that were invaluable in assuring that true transformation and improvement with clinician input was accomplished were:

- **Process Flows:** As part of the design process, the team documented current and ideal states related to the clinical process they were evaluating. For example, with the electronic medication administration build, the team documented the process for administering a medication from the order to documentation.
- **Swim Lanes:** Diagrams that clearly showed items such as role delineation related to those process flows (see Figure 9-1).
- **Start, Stop, Continue Documentation:** A tool that identifies change as it relates to the implementation of a new process by clearly documenting what clinicians will stop doing, continue doing, and start doing. This document is used during design to assure that all aspects of the newly designed process have been addressed, and it proves very helpful with education and adoption.

Each step of the journey toward a fully electronic record and automation has given WellSpan Health experience in creating a meaningful EHR. WellSpan learned from its experiences in order to improve upon the work. Project management brought precision in executing its plans and the tools to assure that clinical process improvement was possible. Clinical involvement and a leadership infrastructure added the necessary resources that yield successful transformation and adoption.

TACKLING ISSUES HEAD ON

As a project is being implemented, inescapably, a variety of issues will surface. Rather than ducking problems, team members should take an active role in working through them. From top leadership to clinicians, everyone is committed to tackling issues, not running from them. Organization-wide, such gritty levels of participation require that everyone buy into system transparency.

If you encounter a problem, don't mask it, which simply adds to the problem. One of the uplifting aspects of a project can be that rather than hiding from issues, and even errors that have been committed, the people involved will bring forth challenges and concerns. This avoids the trap of trying to put a bandaid on a five-inch gash, and it keeps gashes from becoming major wounds.

You have to "get the cards on the table" and work them through. Issues requiring a crucial decision or special handling need to be documented and presented to the appropriate parties. Questions about changes in the system need to be presented to the governance committee. Everything follows a process.

In the early days of one project, several key milestones had been missed. A new project leader was assigned and found a team that had been wrangling for hours about what they "would have, should have, and could have" done. One of the managers at the time was constantly ringing her hands about not having enough resources and not being able to get things done.

After nearly two weeks of observing this approach to challenges, the leader announced the cessation of frequent, unduly long meetings. Instead, meetings would be 30 minutes or less, and the team would stand, rather than sit to create a sense of urgency and to convey that they would not wrangle for hours. They were going to quickly move through the issues, break through barriers, achieve their goals, and move on. The leader also asked for no more recanting about what might have been done. Their collective focus became what they *would do* to stay on track.

The team targeted a milestone only weeks away and emphasized that effective action, not regrets, would enable everyone to succeed. The group was reticent at first, but the leader enforced the message that their meetings, as well as their mission, must stay focused.

Project management surely is not an exact science. Yes, you populate your office with charts and graphs. You do your best to stay on track but, in the end, you're dealing with people who present a variety of challenging situations. You have to respond to the issues as they arise.

Perfection Traps
The quest for perfection can impede progress. In certain aspects of life, such as performing brain surgery or landing a plane, perfection is highly desirable, if not mandatory. Much of life, and much of project implementation, doesn't have to be perfect for things to be fine. You can spend much time and energy seeking perfection, but projects don't proceed perfectly.

Because project management is not an exact science, the ability to stay flexible, anticipate issues, and be open to feedback is critically important. As we have seen, even when starting on shaky ground, as long as you have a plan and measurements, things can turn out for the best.

THE PROJECT STEERING TEAM
Organize and work with a project steering team that examines how resources are being dispensed and determines roadblocks to major issues. Day in and day out, your project steering team serves an important function: It reviews and approves deliverables produced at any time throughout the project. It also resolves issues beyond the authority of the project management team and ensures the commitment of resources the whole way through.

The project steering team is responsible for reviewing project scope changes that, ideally, rarely occur. The project steering team reviews contractual aspects of the project, namely those established with outside vendors and approves, if appropriate, variances to the budget and/or time line. Thus, the project steering team serves as a benign watchdog for the project management team.

Dashboard Updates

The project management team completes and submits weekly project assessments for the project steering team to review. An example of project assessment categories is described next:

Category 1: No identified issues impacting milestones, budget, resources, or quality.

Category 2: Issues identified with potential to impact milestones, budget, resources, or quality.

Category 3: Issues identified that will impact milestones, budget, resources, or quality.

The project management team also prepares a status report, which offers a summary of activities and accomplishments for the prior week and planned activities for the coming week. This report includes any issues and risks identified as well as appropriate comments, the project hours expended for this reporting period, and the project hours projected for the next reporting period. An example project dashboard is shown in Table 9-2.

Expectations

All project team members should be expected to follow and support the project management methodology, employ the work list to manage assigned items, and maintain accurate time reporting, which should be documented in the status report. No project proceeds as smoothly and efficiently as one in which all role players and stakeholders share a common set of expectations. Documenting what your resources are doing helps to tell the story. As referenced earlier, you can't do everything for everybody, and if you can show what your resources are doing and how much capacity is available, it helps manage expectations.

RISKS AND ISSUES

On large projects, things can and do go wrong. Establish some risk management success criteria to serve as guidelines for the duration of the project. The risks, as well as risk mitigation action steps, need to be

Program Area	Last Reported Status	Current Status	Comments
Scope	●	●	Scope has been finalized. Several decision documents completed in the last period.
Schedule	●	●	Design and build is complete. System testing underway.
Budget	▲	▲	As projected, operating budget is at variance due to key activities and Go-Live support. Capital budget is within budget.
Resources	●	▲	Continue to backfill 6 open positions with consulting resources
Issues	●	▲	Issues for current phase continue to be identified & addressed. Training system implementation and potential delays represent a significant risk.
Risks	▲	▲	Concern surrounds physician adoption and Physician Orders gap workflow analysis. A second demo highlighting more complex scenarios is scheduled with two physician executives.
Change Management	●	●	Roll out of Change Management activities are occurring according to plan. Continue to work with facilities on ownership of process and accountability changes.
Communication	●	●	Communication activities are underway.
Benefits	●	●	Benefits Realization reporting continues on a monthly basis. Semi-annual and annual measures will be reported accordingly. Work continues to refine the measures.
Interfaces	●	●	Interface scope has been finalized.
Testing	●	●	Testing activities are on track.
Training	●	●	Curriculum Development and Training Delivery are fully engaged. Knowledge transfer from Design to Training is underway.
Technical	●	●	Demonstration of EHR technologies is planned in the technical Proof of Concept.
Program Management	●	●	All projects progressing according to plan.

Legend

● Indicates function and project area is on track and proceeding according to plan

▲ Indicates function or program area experiencing potential delays and working to mitigate risks

Table 9-2: Dashboard Updates

addressed in a timely manner to diminish their negative impact. Risks have to be documented and communicated appropriately.

If the risk event occurs, it could become an issue that could impact the project time lines and/or budget. Issue management requires documentation, management, and resolution. Resolution represents the conclusion of problems that arose within the project as a result of the issue. Institute a policy to ensure each issue requires a work activity and its own action plan for resolution.

In large-scale EHR projects, issues may not be one-time events. The goal in each case is to raise the issue, document it appropriately, and manage it. Stratify issues based on their relevance to the project:

Low-priority issues do not appear to be on the project's critical path. These are to be solved at once if possible, but they might need to be addressed during subsequent phases in the project.

Medium-priority issues are important to the outcome of the project. These issues need to be resolved if the project is to be completed on time and within budget. Medium-priority issues are assigned a resolution due date. Failing that, the issue should escalate to high priority.

High-priority issues are critical and need to be addressed promptly before the project can proceed. Once an issue is aired, immediate feedback is required from an appropriate authority. The information the authority provides needs to be communicated to the project's sponsor and project management office.

Variations on a Theme

You should rely upon a standard project management template document, wherein the issue is documented as a formal problem statement, followed by a clearly detailed description. The description should delineate who is on top of and who will stay with the issue, and what steps need to be assigned to resolve the issue.

MANAGING ISSUES

Establish four basic success criteria ensuring that issues are:
- Documented, prioritized, and tracked.
- Resolved in a timely manner.
- Escalated appropriately as needed.
- Appropriately communicated in the case of priority issues.

What about when a *change* or *problem* associated with an issue has been identified? In other words, the issue itself changes. In that case, the issue needs to be reviewed including any problems or next steps associated with resolution. Issue-related information, including dates, status, description, and resolution, should be documented for tracking and monitoring.

If an issue owner fails to show suitable progress toward resolving an outstanding issue, then the project manager should follow the prescribed *escalation* process. This process ensures that issues are transparent to the leadership team and, thus, will be appropriately managed.

Sometimes an issue is related to a scope change and is, therefore, considered to be a big deal. In that case, the issue remains documented as an issue until a request for a scope change has been reviewed and approved by the proper governance. If the scope change has been approved, the issue is regarded as closed. The scope change is documented and acknowledged by the project management office. If the scope change is not approved, the decision to not approve, as well as the rationale is documented and the issue is closed.

ERROR MITIGATION STRATEGIES

While EHRs can provide many benefits, unintended consequences from technology implementation could potentially inflict harm by introducing potential "new" errors. The Joint Commission issued a *Sentinel Alert* in December 2008 that stated that organizations "must be mindful of the safety risks and preventable adverse events that these implementations can create or perpetuate."[3]

Unintended Consequences

As sophisticated systems emerge, decreases in medication errors have been observed. Concurrently, such systems can contribute to a rise in other types of errors. In 2005, a study by Koppel et al., published in the *Journal of the American Medical Association*, indicated that CPOE systems could *contribute* to 22 different kinds of medication error risks including information errors encompassing "fragmentation and systems integration failure," and human/machine interface errors encompassing machine rules that don't correctly handle "work organization or usual behaviors." Some of the 22 error risks stemmed from an inability to view on one screen all of a patient's current medications, selecting wrong patients because of alphabetic sorting of patient names, or trying to read a small font size.[4]

In a 2010 *Journal of Healthcare Information Management* article, Sengstack summarized the results of the Koppel study and three others related to the issue of the "potential negative side of CPOE."[5] Another study referenced is that of Campbell et al. in regard to their nine categories of unintended adverse consequences that can occur with CPOE implementations.[6] Sengstack concludes with a CPOE Design Check List that identifies a set of steps for mitigating risks of errors or unintended consequences involved in clinical decision support. Organizations should make sure checklists and tools such as these are part of their design to minimize unintended consequences.

In November 2011, the Insitute of Medicine (IOM) issued a report on the use of health IT and its impact on patient safety. The report recommended creating an oversight structure for tracking patient safety deaths, serious injuries, or potentially unsafe conditions associated with health IT, as well as changes crossing providers, vendors, and policymakers. The IOM also addressed the need for further research to understand safe implementaiton and use of health IT by all users, sociotechnical systems associated with health IT, and the impact of policy decisions on health IT use in clinical practice.[7]

Human factors must be strongly considered when designing and implementing an EHR. The people side of implementation must always be examined in order to make systems as safe as possible. Recognizing that unintended consequences as described earlier can arise in association with EHR implementations, develop an error mitigation strategy for potential errors, including those outlined next by The Joint Commission *Sentinal Alert* and your search of the latest literature.

1. Examine workflow processes and procedures prior to health IT implementation.
2. Actively involve clinicians and staff who will use/be affected by health IT (full life cycle).
3. Assess health IT needs; require IT staff to interact with users outside their facility; reduce interfaces.
4. Continuously monitor health IT for problems; address resultant workarounds/incomplete error reporting early.
5. Provide a training program, including refresher courses, for all types of clinicians and staff; focus on benefits.
6. Create and communicate policies specifying staff authorizations and responsibilities.
7. Prior to taking a technology live, ensure all guidelines/standardized order sets are developed and tested.
8. Develop a graduated system of safety alerts to aid clinicians in determining urgency and relevancy.
9. Mitigate harmful drug orders by requiring department/pharmacy review and sign-off on orders created outside parameters.
10. Provide an environment that protects staff involved in data entry from undue distractions when using health IT.

11. Post-implementation, continue to reassess/enhance safety effectiveness and error-detection capability.
12. Post-implementation, continually monitor/report errors, near misses, or close calls caused by health IT.
13. Reevaluate applicability of security and confidentiality protocols as more medical devices interface with the IT network.[8]

Everyone who participates in the design of the system should also participate in the development of the risk mitigation strategy, and you should communicate this strategy to stakeholders and executives across your health system. Although developing this strategy may require considerable time and resources, it's an essential part of the overall transformation process. Weave this risk mitigation into your overall strategy, and reevaluate periodically as new technology is introduced. Most importantly, have someone in your organization assigned to focus on and be responsible for this work. Typically, this will be a staff person from Risk Management, but they will need Informatics/IT at the table to guide him or her in this work.

CASE STUDY:
PROJECT MANAGEMENT TO
MITIGATE UNFORESEEN CHALLENGES

By Ryan Kennedy, IT Project Manager, Department of Clinical Research Informatics, NIH Clinical Center

INTRODUCTION

The National Institutes of Health (NIH) Clinical Center (CC) is a 240-bed federally-funded, biomedical research hospital in Bethesda, Maryland. The Clinical Center accommodates about 10,000 new patients a year with 95,000 outpatient visits a year. Patients are admitted to the NIH CC from across the world for the sole purpose of participating in clinical research protocols. The Department of Clinical Research Informatics (DCRI) is responsible for the management and development of all CC-owned IT applications, networks, and databases, including the hospital's EMR.

The NIH had been using an EHR since 1976. The system in use was called the Medical Information System (MIS) and was the primary system for all patient encounters at the CC. Although the system was supported by DCRI, new implementations, upgrades, or requests for changes to MIS were assigned without any standard implementation process. Given the unique and varying requirements of the user population, MIS became a highly-customized product with little to no project management or configuration management oversight.

After using the MIS legacy system for over 20 years, a decision was made to upgrade to a new EHR solution. The migration to a new system did not come without risks. Few members of the DCRI participated in the original implementation of MIS, and many lacked experience with implementing new enterprise systems. The project manager of record was the CIO, but given the scope and complexity of this implementation, the CIO delegated the day-to-day management tasks. To ensure a seamless transition, the NIH CC hired a consulting company as the system "Integrator." Their primary role was to ensure all efforts were integrated and completed on time and within budget. They also provided staffing to enhance the existing skill set of the department.

While working closely with the NIH CC CIO, the Integrator followed a standard methodology while focusing on the daily details to ensure everything was completed as planned. Some of the key elements of effective project management were demonstrated throughout the effort, including:

- **Clearly defined roles and responsibilities.** The entire work effort was split up into a "pie," with each piece of the pie given a lead from both the government and vendor. Each piece of the pie was responsible for a portion of the system implementation, which could be likened to program management with multiple-related projects. Once the work was divided and assigned, there were almost 30 pieces of the pie (projects), including clinical documentation, system testing, configuration management, policy review, reports, interfaces, documentation, training, database management, security, communication, activation planning, and application support.

- **The formation of a Project Management Team (PMT).** The PMT, along with the CC senior management, actively supported and monitored the implementation's status. This oversight structure was essential to help manage the scope, budget, and timeliness of work.
- **A detailed project workplan.** Every task and resource required to migrate to the new EMR was documented, along with estimated work effort and duration. This allowed the project team to fully understand what was needed when, and it helped the Integrator to ensure the project was progressing on schedule. In the end, this document stretched to almost 3,000 individual tasks.
- **Regular and appropriate communication.** By setting up a hierarchical support structure and conducting regular weekly meetings among teams, leadership, and stakeholders, everyone on the team was kept well informed of project activities. The outcomes of every meeting were documented with minutes and action items, which were organized in a central repository.
- **Independent Verification and Validation (IV&V).** A contractor was hired to oversee the work being performed to ensure that the system would meet expectations. The IV&V team reviewed all documents created during the project and conducted a complete review of the system configuration as part of their involvement in testing. IV&V was also responsible for risk management for the implementation and developed a risk radar that was reviewed with the project team and stakeholders on a regular basis. An added benefit of IV&V was their leadership role in several rapid design sessions to keep progress moving forward.
- **Activation Checklist.** A detailed activation checklist was developed, which included all activities and tasks that were required in the three days prior to the go-live. It was developed with input from every affected member of the project team and was detailed down to five minute tasks to keep staff on track with what was being done in various locations throughout the hospital.

Through the coordinated efforts of the entire project team, which amounted to almost 200 individuals at a cost of $60 million, a go-live date was set for July 31, 2004. However, as the date approached, testing revealed a problem with the interface engine that could lead to problems loading the historic data from MIS. Given the tight time line, a critical decision had to be made and communicated to the thousands of affected stakeholders who had spent weeks training and adding staff to accommodate the new system. The date was pushed out by three weeks.

Delays and unforeseen events can be expected with any type of project, and IT is not immune. In cases like this, the project manager must ensure that risks, alternatives, and mitigations are presented clearly and accurately, with as much lead time as possible. The project manager also becomes the point of contact for all project-related issues, which is essential when fielding questions and concerns from all levels of the organization. In short, the project manager allows staff to focus on the work they need to do (in this case, fix the interface engine) without having to worry about everything else that may be occurring on the project.

Planning for the unexpected is a trademark of successful project management. Moving forward to the new go-live date in August 2004, the new EHR implementation hit another roadblock in the middle of the activation that required a delay of a full day when staff had already worked through the night. Basic essentials, such as beds and food, were made available for the project staff, while overhead announcements and Clinical Application Field Experts (CAFE) kept hospital staff apprised of the migration's progress. Once again, the project manager was available to oversee the implementation's progress so issues could be fixed in isolation.

In the end, the new EHR system was successfully activated, and today, there is little recollection of the delays or issues that occurred during the go-live. In fact, several components that were developed during the EHR implementation remain to this day, including regular meetings of the PMT group and formal configuration management practices. Perhaps that most significant change to the CC that was borne out of the EHR implementation was the development of a centralized Project Management Office (PMO) within the DCRI.

In conjunction with a reorganization of the DCRI—consolidating technical and clinical staff—the CIO agreed that there was a need for project managers and a standard methodology. The strong support of this leadership, along with the successful outcomes of the EHR implementation, was critical to the initial approval and success of the PMO. Today, the PMO continues to operate and expand, employing four full-time project managers and two business analysts who are responsible for all projects that impact the NIH CC.

REFERENCES

NIH Clinical Center Facts at a Glance. (09/09/2011) Retrieved from http://clinicalcenter.nih.gov/about/welcome/fact.shtml. Accessed May 7, 2012.

Clinical Center News. (January 2003) Retrieved from www.cc.nih.gov/about/news/newsletter/2003/jan03/index.html. Accessed May 7, 2012.

Clinical Center News. (October 2004) Retrieved from www.cc.nih.gov/about/news/newsletter/2004/oct04/index.shtml. Accessed May 7, 2012.

Houston, Susan & Kennedy, Ryan. *Implementing a PMO in a Healthcare Setting.* PMI Global Congress, 8 October 2007.

Garnett, Carla (2001, October 16). New Clinical Research Information System Planned to Replace MIS. *The NIH Record*, 21.

MEETING MANAGEMENT

As project manager and meeting coordinator, it's your responsibility to ensure that the meetings you schedule are of appropriate length, are on target, and represent a forum for the project team to effectively participate, achieve resolution, and further contribute to both short- and long-term project progress.

Meetings are the bane of the professional's existence. Surveys show that most people do not enjoy them, and too many are often subjected to excessive meetings, the value of which could be suspect. On a large-scale implementation project, this might especially be the case.

Dr. Henry Kissinger, Secretary of State under President Richard Nixon, once observed that there was little purpose in having a meeting unless the desired outcomes were known in advance. It may not always be possible to know if desired outcomes can be known in advance, but it is worth adhering to the spirit of his proclamation.

Meeting with your project team (and project role players and stakeholders) is vital to the long-term success of the project. In meetings, everyone communicates in real-time with one another, focuses on objectives, strives for a consensus of opinion, and, ideally, departs feeling re-energized and ready to sharpen the focus on their roles and tasks.

PRESIDING OVER MEETINGS

Employ good meeting management procedures, including issuing agendas 24 hours in advance and issuing minutes within 48 hours following the meeting. The approach to meetings, which mirrors the approach to project management, is to stay within established ground rules, tackle issues one at a time, and let everyone be heard.

As project leaders, week-in and week-out, you should hold meetings with various constituents from within your organization and among your project team. The meetings are designed to present new material, tackle issues, make decisions, or serve as a combination of these functions.

In announcing various aspects of implementation—providing training, offering follow-up, or receiving feedback—you will encounter the same realities of meetings that any host will encounter. This could include less-than-willing participants who shuffle in, shuffle out, then hurry back to what they were doing.

It is inevitable that some people in the meeting will become strong advocates of the system. Others will be resistors. Most people will quickly forget much of what they hear. Some will ask questions. A few will do anything to avoid participation. Whatever meeting participants are asked to do isn't likely to be done on time, or correctly, without follow-up, support, and feedback. So, build that into the system in the form of the super users, advanced super users, SWAT Teams, and so on.

PREPARE, PREPARE, PREPARE

Extensive preparation is the key to conducting meetings that lead to successful systemwide implementations. You should typically spend more time preparing for meetings that you attend, conduct, or otherwise sponsor, than you do *at the meeting itself.* You might shudder at the thought, but this is a reality of effective transformation management.

The amount of time devoted to preparation for a meeting that is ultimately deemed "very productive" by attendees is nearly double the time devoted to meetings that are deemed "not very productive," or "not productive."

The direct benefits of laying this groundwork include having meetings go more effectively, requiring less time, and yielding greater results. Don't be surprised when attendees begin to exhibit enthusiasm for pre-meeting encounters. They feel more valued and as if their input and ideas do matter. Many begin to approach the subsequent meetings with a new and positive perspective.

Pre-meeting discussions also enable you to be a better meeting planner. You're able to create an agenda focused on topics earmarked as important by the group. You can sequence these topics in order, and circulate your agenda in advance, so that attendees arrive with pre-formulated ideas that could benefit the entire group. Also, such advance connections contribute to the odds that your meeting will stay focused, conclude as scheduled, and foster higher participant enthusiasm for subsequent meetings.

For meetings where critical decisions will be made and influential executives will participate, hold a pre-meeting among your team. This serves as a practice session to make sure that you are fully prepared to present crisp, clear, and concise information for effective decision making.

HOW MANY IS TOO MANY?

At one point in a project, one organization noticed an awful lot of meetings being held. They obtained baseline measurements and found that surprisingly, most managers spent over 90 percent of their week in meetings. They wondered how anyone was getting any work done if they were always in one meeting or another. As it turns out, employees were emailing and doing work late at night.

They decided to focus on reducing the number of meetings being held. As a result, they put some key initiatives in place, such as:
• Establishing meeting-free zones.
• Communicating to the team that meetings were needed only for decision making.

- If a meeting was being held to communicate information, it was unnecessary.
- Keeping meetings on time and on focus, with agendas pre-circulated.

By implementing these measures, the aggregate time spent in meetings declined by nearly 60 percent. Large projects can easily create a "meeting craze." Keep an eye on this tendency and coach employees to make optimal use of their time. Also, ensure that scheduled meetings are as productive as possible.

INTERNAL OR EXTERNAL HIRING?

Is it more advantageous to initiate a large transformation management initiative with homegrown talent or with outside help? Both options have their pluses and minuses. For assembling new future-state workflow processes, it might be advantageous for someone from within, who's been there and done that, to provide the guidance and leadership.

Alternatively, even with strong executive leadership, externally hired talent has its advantages. If the organization hasn't been through a major transition process before, external consultants experienced with large transformation initiatives often are better positioned to make many types of requests and deliver some hard messages to key stakeholders.

External hires need to establish relationships with the key veterans who know what buttons to push and how to get people's attention.

In any case, having a leader with major influence and easy command over other people's attention will make it easier to craft the plan and fine-tune the messages.

For smaller organizations that cannot afford to hire one or two full-time project leaders at a competitive salary, review the backgrounds of your staff on board. Who has had formal education, training, or experience in implementing change? The skills and capabilities of those right under your nose might surprise you. Alternatively, can an outside consultant, trainer, or transformation management expert offer assistance? To aid you, checklists and links to toolkits and organizational transformation management surveys are available online at www.cicadvisory.com.

Work-life balance is essential to be able to engage in this kind of work in the first place. With all the preparatory work that you do, you're able to minimize the instances of emergencies and crises. Some will arise, but intense planning has its benefits. As a leader, you should constantly seek to build a strong team and foundation underneath you. You can't be everywhere at all times, but you can grow leaders. You can teach people how to manage the process.

INSIGHTS AND LESSONS LEARNED

- By maintaining a project management office dedicated to the transformation initiative, you're better able to stay on scope, remain on time, and promote effective communication.
- Keep telling the story to all stakeholders and role players, document the resources you've employed, and reinforce for clinicians what's in it for them.
- Extensive preparation is the key to conducting successful meetings; you might spend more time preparing for meetings than the length of the meetings themselves.
- Keep an eye on the number of meetings your team is having, and establish some guideposts to keep the amount of time spent in meetings manageable.
- How clinicians perceive what the system will do for them means everything to them, so you must keep them informed, aligned, and realistic; encourage their enthusiasm but corral their expectations.
- Don't get caught up in perfection—much of project implementation doesn't have to be perfect for things to work out well.
- Technology may introduce new issues that are not anticiapted (unintended consequences). Assign someone in your organziation to be responsible for analyzing and mitigating potential new types of errors.

THINKING FORWARD

1. Have you addressed The Joint Commission's 13 suggested actions, as well as other research findings to support ongoing risk mitigation?
2. Do you have a multi-year budget with support from senior management?
3. How are you managing risks and issues for the EHR implementation?
4. Are you developing your project managers?

REFERENCES

1. Lam W, Chua A. Knowledge Management Project Abandonment: An Exploratory Examination of Root Causes. *Communications of the Association for Information Systems* 2005; 16(35):723-743. http://cais.aisnet.org/articles/16-35/journal.pdf. Accessed September 9, 2011.

2. Evitts A. Why Most Projects Fail. *Breathing Space.* 2011. www.breathing-spaceblog.com/2011/02/why-most-projects-fail.html. Accessed September 9, 2011.

3. Joint Commission. Sentinel Event Alert, December 11, 2008. Safely implementing health information and converging technologies. www.jointcommission.org/assets/1/18/SEA_42.PDF. Accessed July 20, 2011.

4. Koppel R. Metlay JP, Cohen A, Abaluck B, Localio AR, Kimmel SE, Strom BL. Role of computerized physician order entry systems in facilitating medication errors. *JAMA* 2005; 293(10):1197-203.

5. Sengstack P. CPOE Configuration to Reduce Medication Errors. A literature review on the safety of CPOE systems and design recommendations. *J Healthc Inf Manag* 2010; 24(4):26-32.

6. Cambell E, Sittig D, Ash J. Types of unintended consequences related to computerized provider order entry. *J Am Med Inform Assoc* 2006; 13(5):547-556.

7. Health IT and Patient Safety: Building Safer Systems for Better Care. 2008. Institute of Medicine of the National Academies. http://iom.edu/Reports/2011/Health-IT-and-Patient-Safety-Building-Safer-Systems-for-Better-Care.aspx. Accessed January 20, 2012.

8. Safely Implementing Health Information and Converging Technologies. December 11, 2008. The Joint Commission. www.jointcommission.org/assets/1/18/SEA_42.PDF. Accessed January 20, 2012.

CHAPTER 10

Making the Most of Your EHR

INTRODUCTION

Many healthcare organizations rush to implement an EHR and think that the job is finished and they no longer need to focus on improving either the tool or the processes. Implementing an EHR, however, is not a guarantee that improved healthcare quality, safety, or user satisfaction will automatically follow. In fact, EHRs are complex technology systems that can introduce errors, as well as prevent them. Increasingly, EHRs will guide many aspects of patient care—through communication tools, electronic ordering, decision support features, and data management—and the quality of healthcare will often depend on how well they function.[1] Weiner et al. use the term "e-iatrogenesis" to refer to "patient harm caused at least in part by the application of health information technology," and the advent of EHRs will undoubtedly lead to an increase in this phenomenon.[2]

Aside from safety issues, in the rush to comply with Meaningful Use, many may be missing the opportunity to customize EHR systems to their local workflows.[3] Remember that EHR systems are designed before they're actually used. The old adage "You don't know what you don't know" is especially applicable here. Even the well-designed EHR often has elements that don't work as intended. That's why it's important for organizations to constantly seek ways of improving their EHR systems for clinicians, fine-tuning them so they have fewer clicks and improved usability. Some IT executives believe that activating the EHR is the end but, in truth, it's only the beginning of what should turn out to be a never-ending journey.

WHAT OPTIMIZATION CAN ACHIEVE

After implementing your EHR, it's not uncommon to hear statements along the following lines:

- I can't see the patient story.
- I can't find information easily.
- There are too many clicks and it's hard to navigate in the EHR.
- The EHR has too much information. I can't find what's important and what I need to take care of my patients.

Optimization is your opportunity to address these concerns, increase adoption, and improve the benefits your EHR has to offer. One way to achieve this is by focusing on customer service, meaning making it easier for bedside clinicians to deliver high-quality care by leveraging the EHR tools. In today's healthcare environment, clinicians are bombarded by more and more information and demands. Your goal is to maximize your EHR so that they can find information and get the data they need to provide care with fewer clicks.

If this sounds simple, it's not. Data input occurs in many different places in an EHR, and it's often difficult to decipher a patient story and understand what's going on without clicking in a variety of areas within the EHR. Project teams need to think about how to improve usability and offer easier navigation. Even with the most rigorous training program, users don't remember everything they learned, and it's inevitable that they'll add information where it doesn't belong.

This can create problems from both a reporting and a viewing perspective. For example, if you've designed a system to put respiratory rates in a certain data field and a clinician enters them as free text in another data field, that information won't be readily available in the right section of the EHR for rapid clinical decision making. The goal is to improve the quality and consistency of documentation, including ensuring that clinicians are documenting appropriately in terms of regulatory requirements.

Optimization offers an opportunity to offer advanced training after an initial stabilization period, when users are more comfortable with the system. This post-activation period is the time to demonstrate advanced functionality, shortcuts, and other tricks that might not have sunk in the first time around.

It also offers an opportunity to reexamine workflows. Sometimes clinicians will adopt a workaround because the workflow in the system isn't efficient. Optimization is the time to go back and examine some of those workarounds and see what can be done to mitigate them. For example, at one hospital, nurses asked for 20-foot extension cords to scan patients' wristbands because they didn't want to have to move computers into isolation rooms and wipe them down continually. However, because the system was designed to provide safety alerts when wristbands were scanned, this was a problem because the nurses wouldn't be able to see the alerts from 20 feet away. The team needed to come up with another solution, such as putting stationary computers in isolation rooms, to meet the workflow needs. Whether it's a new process or a software modification, the workflow should drive the technology, not the other way around.

FORMULATE A PLAN

As with other EHR implementation strategies, optimization is best achieved one step at a time. You should consider putting together an optimization plan with different phases.

Stabilization

Avoid making any changes to the system for 60 to 90 days after go-live unless there is a financial, patient safety, or regulatory issue. You need to give users plenty of time to acclimate to the new system.

Kick-off

In this phase, designate someone in your organization as the responsible party for optimization. Make sure this role is included in that person's job description. Usually, this would be an informatics director, but it could also be someone in nursing or a physician. There should also be an optimization team that includes workflow experts, system analysts, rule writers, report writers, and perhaps even a Six Sigma Black Belt or Green Belt for analytics. If you have local facility support teams, include them, as well as facility and physician leadership, super users, and clinical educators.

When frontline supervisors and physicians help implement transformative programs such as EHR and ACO programs in a facility and feel as if they have a vested interest, the staff they supervise come to them, not to the project management team, to ask if they are doing the right thing. This is the way it ought to be. Effective transformation occurs one person at a time, on every level of the organization.

Once you've assembled your team, schedule a kick-off to explain what optimization is, why you're doing it, and what you hope to achieve. You should also explain members' roles and responsibilities.

Assess and Analyze

This is the phase in which you gather data. Interview the leadership team and find out what their pain points are. Take a look at the metrics discussed in Chapter 8 to determine if you can identify areas that need improvement. For example, if your CPOE adoption rate is low, that's probably an optimization goal you want to work on. Look at approved workflow processes to find out if there are deviations from the pre-approved versions. Besides metrics, gather data from a variety of sources—rounding reports, service desk tickets, issues logs, interviews, observations—and analyze them.

Implement and Measure

Once you've analyzed the data, create an optimization scorecard or dashboard so you can see what you need to do and prioritize. You will most likely come up with a long list of items, but you won't be able to do everything on the list. Decide what the most important issues are to focus on and develop an action plan and time line around them. You should have collected baseline measurements; go back after 30, 60, and 90 days, look for improvements and use the scorecard to communicate them to your team and stakeholders. Figure 10-1 illustrates a sample scorecard.

Most issues will be related to training, workflow, or the design/ build. For example, suppose your analysis reveals that nurses are not completing blood documentation correctly. The workflow seems to be fine, but they need to be re-educated. You might ask your super users to collect some baseline measurements, providing a form with instructions to audit how many nurses documented blood correctly in a given week. Then have your informatics team prepare a curriculum for additional training to be delivered by your clinical educators and super users. After 30, 60, and 90 days, ask your super users to redo the audits, which should show an improvement. You can now go to the optimization team—the same group with which you had the kick-off—and go over the results.

There are many opportunities for optimization. Some software shows the number of clicks and the time it takes to enter orders. If

Target Metric	Priority	Local/Facility Owner	IT/Informatics Owner	Action Plan	Due Date	Baseline Status	30 Day Measurement	60 Day Measurement	90 Day Measurement
Threshold: 70%, Target 80%, Stretch 90%	HIGH	Dr. John Smith, CMO	Nancy Jones, Sr CPOE Analyst	1. CPOE workgroup to re-evaluate design and workflow 2. Rebuild if applicable post re-evaluation 3. Re-education	2/15/12	⬢	△	△	⬢
Nursing will document CHF education correctly 95%	HIGH	Nancy Nurse, Nursing Director and Sue Smith, Manager of Quality	Jerry Jones, ClinDocTeam Lead	1. Build report-CHF compliance 2. Educate managers and superusers on proper documentation 3. Push report to managers	2/15/12	⬢	⬢	△	⬢

Legend	
⬢	Significantly below established goal; non compliance
◯	Below established goal; at risk for non compliance
⬢	Meets established goal
△	Trending up towards established goal
▽	Trending down; at risk for non compliance

Figure 10-1: Optimization Scorecard

there are physicians who are taking longer or using more clicks, analyze why that's happening, and devise a plan to address it.

Stop-Start-Continue

Keep in mind that many issues will come up; while you may be tempted
to fix every single one, that's not realistic. Together with your optimization team you should focus on key workflows that are the most problematic, deciding which get the highest priority. Physicians want to
know three things: what's different, how the process affects them, and
what they need to do to make it better. Tell them clearly and concisely
what they need to stop doing, what they need to start doing, and what
will continue unchanged to make things better.

ENHANCED TRAINING

Optimization affords an opportunity to re-engage your super users and
offer enhanced training. Since physician training tends to take place at
the elbow, survey your physician champions to determine areas where
physicians are struggling and what you can teach them that will ease
the way in adopting the new system. Create a list of topics and ask your
informatics or facility support team to collaborate with high-impact/
high-volume physicians, spending time with them during rounds or
perhaps holding an information session in the physician lounge. Be

innovative in figuring out a way to reach physicians in order to teach them tips and tricks that will save them time.

Other Opportunities

- It's worthwhile to consider doing a mock Joint Commission survey before an accreditation visit, ideally about three to six months prior to a visit. This allows you to incorporate the survey results into your optimization plan.
- Engaging and compensating your staff is another opportunity to maximize optimization and adoption. Some organizations have a skills ladder, or you might consider adding optimization goals to manager or employee performance goals. Think about how to leverage any bonus incentives or performance improvements in support of your optimization plan so that users are constantly working to improve the EHR.

INCREASING USABILITY

Improving the usability of EHR tools requires a cooperative effort with the vendor. Your quest is to create a one-stop shopping system for the clinicians, so that they can access the system and serve patients more ably. This is best achieved when they have in-depth access to their patients' EHR. Ultimately, the goal is to achieve a high level of usability by clinicians, so that adoption becomes firmly entrenched.

Without high adoption of basic system functions, you're going to have a difficult time employing other system tools that could help people accomplish their tasks more efficiently.

You might encounter others within your organization, such as those using Google Health or other widely available software applications, who are puzzled and ask, "Why can't we do this yet?" You will not have a solution for them, but don't let that deter your efforts. Everyone in healthcare is on a journey to assemble basic tools to take care of patients and improve quality and safety.

By mastering and optimizing your EHR, you can position your organization to take advantage of alerts and prompts that will yield advanced clinical decision support and ultimately improved outcomes.

When clinical decision support is fully established, you will be able to receive intelligent alerts automatically. For example, if a patient has a blood pressure of X, a lab result of Y, and another test indicating Z, the intelligent alerts inform the clinician that the patient is at high risk of going into septic shock. The clinician who is interrupted 15 times a day doesn't have time to sit down and focus on patterns in patient data that likely are cause for concern. By using the intelligent processes within systems to receive alerts via a smart phone or other mobile device, the clinician is empowered in unprecedented ways. Many organizations in the United States have such alerts in place and have reduced mortality rates. With a population base of as few as 100 patients, consider how many lives could be saved.

AVOIDING ERRORS AFTER THE HEAVY LIFTING

In healthcare today, especially nursing, many employees leave within a few years. Hospitals have a variety of inexperienced clinicians in the workforce. Intelligent alert systems augment the skills of less experienced nurses and of the organization's workforce in general.

With today's technology, you can put indicators in place to prevent the occurrence of tragic events that could have been prevented. You can alert the clinician early when a problem arises. Such technology can make a dramatic difference in the quality of care, especially in an environment of constant turnover. But just because you have the ability to establish these alerts doesn't mean you should introduce one hundred of them at once. If you do, you will overwhelm and fatigue your clinicians. They won't be able to pay attention to each alert.

In terms of patient safety, there are many lessons to be learned from the U.S. airline industry. Many challenges have been noted in the past with aircraft cockpit instrumentation and engineering design in terms of pilot interaction that could lead to increased risk of confusion.[4] That being said, it has also been noted that "passenger deaths aboard major U.S. airlines hit a total of zero (2001 to 2006), yet American hospitals killed an estimated 250,000 to 500,000 patients with medical mistakes in that same five-year period."[5] It's clear that healthcare can benefit from these lessons learned and understand the importance of alert fatigue and the work that still remains to incorporate alerts properly in the EHR.

It's crucial to stay focused on the key clinical issues that you identified and develop intelligent alerts around them. Then you can measure the outcomes to determine if you're actually making a difference.

Introduce other tools and measures of control in a manner that people can comfortably absorb and apply, *after* a system is up and running, and only when clinicians are proficient with it. Establishing the base represents the heavy lifting. Once you've activated your facility and moved into post-activation strategies, you have something to build on. It becomes a matter of building upon the information you have and translating it into even more meaningful information. Remember, it's easier to double an existing knowledge base than to have created the base in the first place. Millionaires will tell you that earning the first million was tough, but earning the second million was considerably easier.

DEMOGRAPHIC AND NEED SHIFTS

Within a few years, one fifth of the U.S. population will be age 65 or older. This is noteworthy because people in this age group employ healthcare resources at twice the rate of those younger than 65. Many consumers in this age category have chronic conditions for which they seek care. Concurrently, a large segment of the population continues to gain weight, and the variety of ailments and conditions associated with obesity will prompt a demand for healthcare services unknown in previous generations.

Fewer people are visiting primary care providers, and yet we believe that the role of the primary care provider must expand, not contract. With the proper incentives in place, as discussed in Chapter 1, perhaps more medical students and interns will be attracted to primary care.

Along with the rise in the number of seniors and overweight people, paradoxically, more individuals than ever before seek an active, healthy lifestyle, some well into their later years. This will prompt unprecedented demands for sports medicine and orthopedic surgeries, such as knee and hip replacements.[6]

A distinct segment of healthcare consumers will take full responsibility for their health and will be aptly assisted by access and control of their personal health records. Equal numbers of healthcare consumers are likely to assume a passive role, preferring to follow traditional models, wherein physicians, nurses, and health advisors tell them exactly what to do for what ails them. The large middle area will consist of consumers who assume a fair share of responsibility for their health, particularly when confronted by accidents, illness, or harrowing incidents that shake them into taking action.

The innovators and early adopters will soon possess and maintain their own data; however, one day, a majority of patients will possess and maintain their own data. It is still early on the adoption curve.

All three of the groups discussed represent your potential customer base. All three will be aptly served by the EHR that you implement. When installed and employed effectively, information technology improves the quality of patient care, your facility's profitability, and your standing within your market for health services. Meanwhile, the nature of the industry is about to be turned on its head.

YOUR CONSUMER-CENTRIC FUTURE

Rather than risk being caught off-guard by the coming revolution in healthcare delivery systems, recognize that with tremendous upheaval lies the seeds of significant opportunity. Customers' wants and desires will drive the industry and help determine which providers succeed or fail, so healthcare leaders everywhere need to adopt a forward-thinking posture.

When Customers Rule

Customers will be predisposed to patronizing only transparent organizations. As CMS moves forward with instituting value-based purchasing programs, and commercial payers continue to evolve their own incentive-based models, these organizations will represent those that have achieved Meaningful Use and have comparison data readily available. Such providers will have implemented and optimized a system-wide EHR and thoroughly embraced IT, and will rely upon personal EHRs to fuel their business and streamline operations.

Healthcare providers are preparing for the day when typical consumers will be more knowledgeable about health plans and health choices than ever before. Their preferences as to how they learn about your facility or organization and how they gather information, including audio, text, video, graphics, referrals, and recommendations will ultimately impact who and how many you serve, what procedures you offer, and your potential for a long-term relationship with patients.

No provider can ignore that consumers have a variety of choices unlike anything witnessed by previous generations. From medical boutiques to convenience care facilities to medical tourism, every facility will find itself in competition from all corners of the state, region, and globe.

THE CHALLENGE FOR YOUR TEAM

Your challenge is to embrace the industry as it unfolds, not shrink from it. Your mission is to capitalize on your facility's brand, services, and reputation. By achieving notable improvements in the delivery of patient care, as evidenced by suitably employed metrics, you can establish or maintain a strong foothold in your target market. As word spreads that you consistently offer unsurpassed quality of individualized patient care, people will seek you out.

The transformation initiatives you implement must result in demonstrably consistent performance from facility to facility, department to department, and with patient after patient. Your executive team and all role players need to understand that delivering the highest quality patient care will be sacrosanct.

More patients will become avid consumers—predisposed to heavy comparison-shopping—with a wide array of healthcare choices before them. So, when an exemplary local provider emerges from their search, why wouldn't customers want to stay close to home? Your mission is to preempt the local marketplace and become the default option because it makes perfect sense for customers to bring their business to you.

Maintaining the Proper Outlook

Surmising that a mere six to twelve months of pain will suffice to make the transition to Meaningful Use will bring more trouble than you can imagine. Maintain a long-term outlook with adequate time horizons. You have to walk before you can run.

Healthcare needs will not dry up. They will evolve, and you can be positioned to accommodate the digital age and era of accountable care in the twenty-first century. Regardless of what reforms and legislation are handed down by government, the cost of healthcare will continue to rise, as the value of the dollar decreases and customer expectations increase. Even if you represent a small, single facility with limited resources, acknowledge the fundamentals of your situation.

Implementing an effective EHR system and making good on the promise of information technology within your facility or organization will help counterbalance rising costs, or at least diminish their trajectory. Applying these same principles in the implementation of public and private accountable care programs will help overcome the organizational and technological challenges that come with the new model of care delivery. Ultimately, providers who effectively harness the power of technology and embrace the new requirements to be more accountable for the care delivered will enjoy a huge competitive edge over others.

Transformation will *not* occur in the absence of optimal use of IT. The coordination of patient care, staff resources, enhanced reporting and billing, and a consistent facility or organization-wide increase in quality cannot be achieved without a centralized way of capturing, monitoring, analyzing, and applying the data.

Rather than reacting in a piecemeal fashion to individual health-care needs, an expertly implemented and optimized EHR will enable you to pursue an expansive, all-encompassing approach to quality patient care. There is no substitute for this.

THE PAYOFF IS IN THE WORKS

Reforms in the health insurance market will result in greater demand for high-quality healthcare services than can be readily met, at least locally or regionally. Coupled with restrictions providers might face in serving patients, demand might well exceed supply. Consider how you can capitalize on such a scenario, because the transformation initiative that you undertake to meet the challenges previously outlined might take years before a facility's profitability rises as a result. You'll likely need offsetting revenue streams.

At first, new instructions, procedures, methods of administration, and constant maintenance will challenge you and your facility's staff in unprecedented ways. Think about the introduction of other technology and what kinds of productivity and profitability gains companies were able to achieve. In the case of the personal computer, productivity gains were not widely evident for at least a decade. More than two decades later, the enhanced productivity that we all enjoy daily is a given. We wouldn't think of proceeding without such technology.

In the short run, as you implement an EHR to support the next generation of care delivery, some productivity and profitability gains might accrue as a result of eliminating redundancies, reducing waste, and decreasing the incidence of misdirected efforts. The long and winding road upon which your facility embarks will result in a more streamlined mode of operations across all departments. This leaner, more efficient system ultimately will yield strategic and competitive advantages.

BE AMONG THE LEADERS

It's unclear how many healthcare organizations will have fully converted to EHR systems by the middle of the decade. By some forecasts, it will be one in four facilities; by others, as many as three in four. Something closer to the middle is more likely. With the implementation of health-care reform, both public and private, accountability for the quality of patient care is at a critical juncture. An effective EHR implementation is an underpinning for clinically integrated organizations and account-able care. With transparency required in clinical quality performance reporting, the application of lessons learned and best practices shared in this book can be of value to stakeholders throughout the industry.

From the standpoint of your facility, coming late to the table yields little value and adds much risk. With IT destined to become the decid-ing factor for which facilities thrive and which fall by the wayside, the time to take action is now. In 2001, the Institute of Medicine issued its report on *Crossing the Quality Chasm*. It outlined not only the often mentioned six aims for high quality care but also rules for redesign-ing and improving care, and underlying reasons for inadequate quality of care.[7] One of these reasons was the growing complexity of science and technology. Ten years later, we can look toward the horizon and see that the pace of change has only accelerated as we have more tech-nology being developed at an increasingly rapid pace, bringing new tools to market on a daily basis. As healthcare leaders today and for the future generation, you have a duty to bring the full benefits of new sys-tems to care settings to benefit patients, physicians, nurses, and other healthcare workers across the United States.

Despite the frustration, confusion, and sometimes exasperation, putting your stake in the ground now is the only strategy that makes sense. You owe it to every patient who walks in your front doors to help them depart healthier than when they arrived.

INSIGHTS AND LESSONS LEARNED

- Implementing an EHR does not guarantee that improved quality, safety, or user satisfaction will automatically follow.
- Develop an optimization plan using a phased approach that allows you to identify and address concerns.
- Never assume that managers can simply receive a set of instructions and then be left to handle everything on their own. Return to them

again and again to reinforce what you've already provided and to support them in ways that they indicate they need.

- Patients want to stay close to home, especially when they have an exemplary local provider. Preempt the local marketplace and become their default provider.
- The arduous road your facility or organization travels when implementing an EHR ultimately will result in streamlined operations across all departments.

CLOSING POINTS

- Committed corporate and local executives create a viable climate for transformation.
- Setting and communicating realistic goals, expectations, and accountability measures are the keys to effective leadership.
- Clinicians must own the system design, implementation, redesigned workflow, and standardization.
- Recognize and constantly measure levels of resistance to transformation.
- Clinicians need to serve as the system's "disciples," marketing the successes of the organization internally.
- Appreciate the fact that transformation management requires more effort than system design.
- Recognize that learning is both a continuous and mutual experience.

REFERENCES

1. Hoffman S, Podgurski A. Meaningful Use and Certification of Health Information Technology: What About Safety? [Supplement]. *J Law Med Ethics* 2011;March (39).

2. Weiner J, Kfuri T, Chan K, et al. "e-Iatrogenesis": The most critical unintended consequence of CPOE and other HIT. *J Am Med Inform Assoc* 2007; 14(3), 387-388.

3. Sittig D, Classen D. Safe electronic health record Use requires a comprehensive monitoring and evaluation rramework. *JAMA* 2010; 303(5), 450-451.

4. Jarrett DN. Crewstation Design. *Cockpit Engineering*. Burlington, VT: Ashgate Publishing Company; 2005:77.

5. Nance J. *Why Hospitals Should Fly. The Ultimate Flight Plan for Patient Safety and Quality Care.* Bozeman, MT: Second River Healthcare Press; 2008:28.

6. Centers for Disease Control and Prevention (CDC). Vital signs: state-specific obesity prevalence among adults—United States, 2009. *MMWR* 2010 Aug 6; 59(30):951-955.

7. Institute of Medicine, Committee on Quality of Health Care in America. Chapter 1: A new health system for the 21st century and Chapter 3: Formulating new rules to redesign and improve care. In: *Crossing the Quality Chasm: A New Health System for the 21st Century.* Washington, DC: National Academies Press; 2001:23-33, 61-88.

Project/Change Management Gurus

Project management in general and change management as a discipline arose after the Japanese surrender in World War II. Industrial societies and organizations needed outside help from management consultants to improve manufacturing operations, increase product quality, and raise customer satisfaction levels. Throughout the book, we referenced Harvard University Professor John Kotter, as his philosophy was drawn upon to help guide our own change management practices. In this appendix, we have provided a synopsis of some of the other leading project management and change management thought leaders in modern history. W. Edwards Deming was among the first and most widely acclaimed.

W. Edwards Deming, PhD and the Quest for Quality

W. Edwards Deming (1900–1993), author, educator, lecturer, consultant, and pioneer of the quality change movement, had an enormous impact on American change management in all areas of business. He is perhaps most famous for his work with Japanese managers and engineers post-World War II. After receiving a medal of honor from the Japanese government and later gaining acclaim in the U.S for his contribution to rebuilding the Japanese economy, Dr. Deming was honored with the National Medal of Technology by President Reagan in 1987. His books include *Quality, Productivity, and Competitive Position* (1982), *The New Economics* (1984), and *Out of the Crisis* (1986).

Quality Defined – Dr. Deming believed that quality cannot effectively be defined by a broad set of terms that stretches over many disciplines; it is a concept that must be defined and distinguished by the customer for specific tasks. Through collecting and analyzing statistical information about reducing the variation among an organization's processes and products, Dr. Deming developed the "14 Points for Management" as a guide for quality improvement. To endure changes to production and service, he taught that improvements must occur on a continual basis and not be handled by setting timeframes for individual improvements.

Management Leaders – Dr. Deming believed that because of the unfamiliar economic age following World War II, Western management officers in companies and organizations needed to aggressively conduct and manage transformation. Dr. Deming felt it beneficial to define organizations, to these officers, as systems composed of networks, with hierarchies of smaller systems.

Joseph Juran

Joseph Juran (1904–2008) worked as an engineer, university professor, corporate director, government administrator, management consultant, and industrial executive. In 1945, Juran quit his job of 25 years with Western Electric and dedicated his efforts to developing and promulgating the study of quality in business. After about a decade of research on the topic, Juran presented his synergistic impact of quality theory to Japanese business leaders. Like Dr. Deming, he was honored by the Japanese government for his economic contributions.

Totality – Juran's work is categorized as "total quality management" in contrast to Deming's work, which is categorized as "quality improvement." Juran founded the Juran Institute in 1979 to study quality in business. His institute taught that quality was "fitness for use" and that progress toward new, advanced levels of business performance in quality management were called "breakthroughs." His books include *Juran on Planning for Quality* (1988) and *The Quality Control Handbook* (1988).

Balancing Control and Breakthrough – Juran studied management projects separately and advocated finding a balance between the effort and time spent on expanding a product's special features versus eliminating flaws of a product. It is vital for managers to find a balance between using control to maintain current levels of performance while preventing harmful changes and striving for quality breakthroughs.

Managers often increase their control to overcome resistance to the changes that come with industry breakthroughs, even when such breakthroughs can increase an organization's long-term prosperity. Some control measures, however, have a short-term focus and can hinder breakthrough activities that lead to innovation.

Juran associated breakthroughs and controls with highs and lows in performance, believing that integration of this constant cycle of highs and lows into a management system promotes ongoing benefits to the total quality of an organization.

Philip B. Crosby

Philip B. Crosby has worked as an engineer and quality expert. He devised the "Zero Defects" concept as director of quality and corporate vice president of ITT at the Martin Marietta Corporation, where he worked for 14 years. He is the author of *Quality is Free* (1979), *Quality Without Tears* (1984), and *Leading* (1990).

All or Nothing – Defining quality as conformance to requirements, Crosby believed that either quality exists completely or does not exist at all, without levels in between, and that communicating expectations for quality of production and service provides rational, realistic requirements that produce desired results. He proposed the following formula to allow managers to quantify the cost of making mistakes:

Cost of Quality = Price of Conformance (the cost of doing things right the first time) + Price of Nonconformance (the cost of waste incurred by error)

Zero Defect – This concept suggests that if products are made correctly at the onset, the price of nonconformance, and thus, the overall cost of quality, can be reduced. This notion requires perfection the first time from every individual in an organization. Crosby focused on identifying preventative measures to avoid errors, rather than seeking efficient means to fix errors once they occurred.

Robert Blake, PhD, and Jane Mouton

In 1961, Robert Blake, PhD, and Jane Mouton began marketing a grid tool they developed for describing managerial leadership styles through Scientific Methods, a company they founded in Austin, Texas. Their now famous "managerial grid" received widespread attention and profoundly influenced corporate America. Their books include *The Managerial Grid: Key Orientations for Achieving Production Through People* (1965), *The Managerial Grid: The Key to Leadership Excellence* (1985), and *Change by Design* (1989).

Grid Lock – To assess a particular manager's leadership style, a questionnaire must first be administered to measure the intensity of the manager's concern with people and production. These are the two primary areas of management responsibility.

After the questionnaire is completed, two scores are administered and then plotted on the grid to describe the manager's leadership style. A score of one reveals that the manager places little or no importance on the principle being measured; a score of nine shows that the manager regards the principle with high importance.

Managerial Types – Four extreme scores, as well as mid-range scores such as 5.5, are possible. In the following descriptions, the first number corresponds to the manager's concern with production, and the second number corresponds to his or her concern with people.

- **1,9 Country Club Management:** Attention is given to the needs of people, leading to satisfying interpersonal relationships, a comfortable work tempo, and a friendly organizational atmosphere.
- **1,1 Impoverished Management:** Minimum exertion to accomplish required work is appropriate to sustain organization membership.
- **5,5 Organization Management:** Adequate organization performance is possible by maintaining team morale at a satisfactory level and harmonizing the need to work.
- **9,1 Authority-Obedience:** Efficiency in operations results from arranging conditions of work as to keep human interference at a minimum.
- **9,9 Team Management:** Highly productive work execution is seen from dedicated people; interdependence through a "common stake" in the organization leads to relationships of trust and respect within the organization's team.

Objectivity – Dr. Blake commented that most people would not be sufficiently aware to be able to place themselves accurately on such a grid. This lack of self-awareness leads to incorrect assumptions about where one might stand on this trait grid, leading to negative direct implications for change managers.

Dr. Blake argued that "a tremendous amount of self-deception enters into this raw, naïve self examination... as long as you are deceiving yourself, any plan of personal change is likely to be invalid." Thus, although it might not be easy, it is important to see oneself objectively to ensure successful managerial change and overall effectiveness.

REFERENCES

Blake R, Mouton J. *The Managerial Grid: Key Orientations for Achieving Production Through People.* Houston: Gulf Publishing Company; 1965.

Blake R, Mouton J. *The Managerial Grid: The Key to Leadership Excellence.* Houston: Gulf Publishing Company; 1985.

Blake R, Mouton J. *Change by Design.* Upper Saddle River, New Jersey: Prentice Hall; 1989.

Crosby P. *Quality is Free: The Art of Making Quality Certain.* New York: Mentor; 1979.

Crosby P. *Quality Without Tears: The Art of Hassle-Free Management.* New York: McGraw Hill; 1984.

Crosby P. *Leading: The Art of Becoming an Executive.* New York: McGraw Hill; 1989.

Deming WE. *Quality Productivity and Competitive Position.* Cambridge: Massachusetts Institute of Technology; 1982.

Deming WE. *The New Economics for Industry, Government, Education.* Cambridge: The MIT Press; 1984.

Deming WE. *Out of the Crisis.* Cambridge: Massachusetts Institute of Technology; 1982.

Juran JM. *Juran on Planning for Quality.* New York: The Free Press; 1988.

Juran JM. *Juran's Quality Control Handbook.* New York: McGraw Hill; 1988.

Appendix B

Further Reading

Arlotto PW, Birch PC, Irby SP. *Beyond Return on Investment: Expanding the Value of Healthcare Information Technology*. Chicago: Healthcare Information and Management Systems Society, 2007.

Barlow J. *A Complaint is a Gift*. San Francisco, CA: Berrett-Koehler, 1996.

Berry L, Seltman K. *Management Lessons from Mayo Clinic: Inside One of the World's Most Admired Service Organizations*. New York: McGraw-Hill, 2008.

Bower AG. *The Diffusion and Value of Healthcare Information Technology*. Santa Monica, CA: Rand Corp., 2006.

Christensen CM. *The Innovator's Dilemma: The Revolutionary Book that Will Change the Way You Do Business*. New York: Harper Paperbacks, 2003.

Christensen CM. *The Innovator's Prescription: A Disruptive Solution for Health Care*. New York: McGraw-Hill, 2008.

Christensen CM, Horn MB, Johnson CW. *Disrupting Class: How Disruptive Innovation Will Change the Way the World Learns*. New York: McGraw-Hill, 2008.

Christensen CM. Raynor ME. *The Innovator's Solution: Creating and Sustaining Successful Growth*. Cambridge, MA: Harvard Business Press, 2003.

Einbinder L. *Transforming Health Care Through Information: Case Studies (Health Informatics)*. New York: Springer, 2009.

Gawande A. *The Checklist Manifesto*. New York: Metropolitan Books, 2009.

Gladwell M. *The Tipping Point*. New York: Bay Back Books, 2002.

Graban M. *Lean Hospitals: Improving Quality, Patient Safety, and Employee Satisfaction*. New York: Productivity Press, 2008.

Holger R, Kotter J. *Our Iceberg Is Melting: Changing and Succeeding Under Any Conditions*. New York: St. Martin's Press, 2005.

Konschak C, Jarrell L. *Consumer-Centric Healthcare: Opportunities and Challenges for Providers*. Chicago: ACHE Publishing, 2011.

Kropf R, Scalzi G. *Making Information Technology Work: Maximizing the Benefits for Health Care Organizations*. Chicago: Health Forum, AHA Press, 2007.

Nance J. *Why Hospitals Should Fly. The Ultimate Flight Plan for Patient Safety and Quality Care*. Bozeman, MT: Second River Healthcare Press, 2008.

Robert L. *Breakthrough Business Meetings*. Avon, MA: Adams Media, 1994.

Peter P, Vohr E. *Safe Patients, Smart Hospitals: How One Doctor's Checklist Can Help Us Change Health Care from the Inside Out*. New York: Hudson Street Press, 2010.

Charlotte AW, Delaney CW, Carr RL, et al. *Nursing and Informatics for the 21st Century: An International Look at Practice, Trends and the Future*. Chicago: HIMSS, 2006.

Managing complex change. Villa RA, Thousand JS (eds.). In: *Creating An Inclusive School*. Alexandria, VA: Association for Supervision & Curriculum Development. 2005.

Web Resources

American Nursing Informatics Association-Caring (ANIA-CARING)
www.ania-caring.org.
ANIA-CARING provides information on research, education, communication, professional activites, and networking within the field of nursing informatics.

AMIA
www.amia.org/
AMIA aims to lead the way in transforming healthcare through trusted science, education, and the practice of informatics and serves as the bridge for knowledge and collaboration across a continuum, from basic and applied research to the consumer and public health arenas.

Association of Medical Directors of Information Systems (AMDIS)
www.amdis.org/
AMDIS is the premier professional organization for physicians interested in and responsible for healthcare information technology.

College of Healthcare Information Management Executives (CHIME)
www.cio-chime.org/
CHIME serves the professional development needs of healthcare CIOs, advocating the more effective use of information management within healthcare.

Healthcare Information and Management Systems Society (HIMSS)
www.himss.org
HIMSS provides information on global leadership for the optimal use of information technology and management systems for the betterment of healthcare.

Institute for Healthcare Improvement (IHI)
www.ihi.org
IHI is an independent not-for-profit organization that focuses on motivating and building the will for change; identifying and testing new models of care in partnership with both patients and healthcare professionals; and ensuring the broadest possible adoption of best practices and effective innovations.

Institute of Medicine of the National Academies
www.iom.edu
The Institute of Medicine is the health arm of the National Academy of Sciences that asks and answers the nation's most pressing questions about health and healthcare.

Appendix D

Journal Articles and Reports

Blumenthal D, Tavenner M. The meaningful use regulation for electronic health records. *N Engl J Med* 2010; 363(6):501-504.

Cambell E, Sittig D, Ash J. Types of unintended consequences related to computerized provider order entry. *J Am Inform Assoc* 2006; 13(5):547-556.

Centers for Disease Control and Prevention (CDC). Vital signs: state-specific obesity prevalence among adults—United States, 2009. *MMWR* 2010;59(30):951-955.

Congressional Budget Office, Report on Evidence on the Costs and Benefits of Health Information Technology. May 2008.

DeVore S, Figlioli K. Lessons premier hospitals learned about implementing electronic health records. *Health Aff (Millwood)*. 2010; 29(4):664-667.

Eber MR, Laxminarayan R, Perencevich EN, et al. Clinical and economic outcomes attributable to health care-associated sepsis and pneumonia. *Arch Intern Med* 2010 Feb 22;170(4):347-353.

Ford EW, Menachemi N, Peterson LT, et al. Resistance is futile: but it is slowing the pace of EHR adoption nonetheless. *J Am Med Inform Assoc* 2009; 16(3):274-281.

Goldstein J. Big challenges await health-records transition. *Wall Street Journal*. April 21, 2009.

HIT Policy Committee Meaningful Use Workgroup. Two Hearings on MU Criteria. http://healthit.hhs.gov/portal/server. pt/community/healthit_hhs_gov__home/1204

Institute of Medicine, Committee on Quality of Health Care in America. *Crossing the Quality Chasm: A New Health System for the 21st Century.* Washington, DC: National Academies Press; 2001.

Institute of Medicine, Committee on Quality of Health Care in America. *To Err Is Human.* Washington, DC: National Academies Press; 2000.

Jha A, DesRoches C, Campbell E. Use of electronic health records in U.S. hospitals. *N Engl J Med* 2009; 360(16):1628-1638.

Joint Commission *Sentinel Event Alert*, Report on Safely Implementing Health Information and Converging Technologies. Issue 42, December 2008.

Klevens RM, Edwards JR, Richards CL Jr, et al. Estimating health care-associated infections and deaths in U.S. hospitals, 2002. *Public Health Rep* 2007 Mar-Apr;122(2):160-166.

Koppel R, Metlay JP, Cohen A, et al. Role of computerized physician order entry systems in facilitating medication errors. *JAMA* 2005; 293(10):1197-1203.

Lam W, Chua A. Knowledge management project abandonment: an exploratory examination of root causes. *Communications of the Association for Information Systems* 2005; 16(35):723-743. http://cais.aisnet.org/articles/16-35/journal.pdf.

Maryland Health Commission Report, The Importance of Electronic Health Record Training. June 2010.

McGillis HL, Pedersen C, Fairley L. Losing the moment: Understanding interruptions to nurses' work. *J Nurs Adm.* 2010; 40(4):169-176.

Sengstack P. CPOE Configuration to reduce medication errors. A literature review on the safety of CPOE systems and design recommendations. *JHIM* 2010; 24(4):26-32.

Thompson DI, Osheroff J, Classen D, et al. Review of methods to estimate the benefits of EMRs in hospitals and the need for a national benefits database. *J Healthc Inf Manag* 2007; 21(1):62-68.

Zhou L, Soran C, Jenter C. The relationship between electronic health record use and quality of care over time. *JAMIA* 2009; 16(4).

Appendix E

Acronyms Used in This Book

ACO	Accountable Care Organization
ARRA	American Recovery and Reinvestment Act of 2009
CIO	Chief Information Officer
CMO	Chief Medical Officer
CNO	Chief Nursing Officer
CPOE	Computerized Provider Order Entry
CMS	Department of Health and Human Services' Centers for Medicare & Medicaid Services (CMS)
ED	Emergency Department
EHR	Electronic Health Record
FST	Facility Steering Team
HAI	Hospital-Acquired Infection
HITECH	Health Information Technology for Economic and Clinical Health Act
ICU	Intensive Care Unit
NICU	Neonatal Intensive Care Unit
OB	Obstetrics
OR	Operating Room
OTT	Organizational Transformation Team
VPMA	Vice President of Medical Affairs

Index

"*f*" next to page number denotes a Figure
"*t*" next to page number denotes a Table